OPPOSING VIEWPOINTS® SERIES

NASA

Other Books of Related Interest:

Opposing Viewpoints Series

The Federal Budget

National Service

The U.S. Intelligence Community

At Issue Series

The Federal Budget Deficit

What Is Humanity's Greatest Challenge?

Current Controversies Series

Nuclear Energy

Patriotism

"Congress shall make no law . . . abridging the freedom of speech, or of the press."

First Amendment to the US Constitution

The basic foundation of our democracy is the First Amendment guarantee of freedom of expression. The Opposing Viewpoints series is dedicated to the concept of this basic freedom and the idea that it is more important to practice it than to enshrine it.

OPPOSING VIEWPOINTS® SERIES

NASA

Margaret Haerens, Book Editor

GREENHAVEN PRESS
A part of Gale, Cengage Learning

GALE
CENGAGE Learning®

Detroit • New York • San Francisco • New Haven, Conn • Waterville, Maine • London

GALE
CENGAGE Learning®

Elizabeth Des Chenes, *Managing Editor*

For more information, contact:
Greenhaven Press
27500 Drake Rd.
Farmington Hills, MI 48331-3535
Or you can visit our Internet site at gale.cengage.com

Articles in Greenhaven Press anthologies are often edited for length to meet page requirements. In addition, original titles of these works are changed to clearly present the main thesis and to explicitly indicate the author's opinion. Every effort is made to ensure that Greenhaven Press accurately reflects the original intent of the authors. Every effort has been made to trace the owners of copyrighted material.

LIBRARY OF CONGRESS CATALOGING-IN-PUBLICATION DATA

NASA / Margaret Haerens, book editor.
p. cm. -- (Opposing viewpoints) Summary: "NASA: Opposing Viewpoints is the leading source for libraries and classrooms in need of current-issue materials. The viewpoints are selected from a wide range of highly respected sources and publications"-- Provided by publisher.
Includes bibliographical references and index.
ISBN 978-0-7377-5745-3 (hardback) -- ISBN 978-0-7377-5746-0 (paperback)
1. United States. National Aeronautics and Space Administration. 2. Outer space--Exploration--United States. 3. Astronautics--United States. I. Haerens, Margaret.
TL521.312.N333 2012
629.40973--dc23
2011041915

Printed in the United States of America
1 2 3 4 5 6 7 16 15 14 13 12

Contents

Chapter 4: What Role Should NASA Play in Diplomatic and Scientific Affairs?

Why Consider Opposing Viewpoints?

> *"The only way in which a human being can make some approach to knowing the whole of a subject is by hearing what can be said about it by persons of every variety of opinion and studying all modes in which it can be looked at by every character of mind. No wise man ever acquired his wisdom in any mode but this."*
>
> *John Stuart Mill*

In our media-intensive culture it is not difficult to find differing opinions. Thousands of newspapers and magazines and dozens of radio and television talk shows resound with differing points of view. The difficulty lies in deciding which opinion to agree with and which "experts" seem the most credible. The more inundated we become with differing opinions and claims, the more essential it is to hone critical reading and thinking skills to evaluate these ideas. Opposing Viewpoints books address this problem directly by presenting stimulating debates that can be used to enhance and teach these skills. The varied opinions contained in each book examine many different aspects of a single issue. While examining these conveniently edited opposing views, readers can develop critical thinking skills such as the ability to compare and contrast authors' credibility, facts, argumentation styles, use of persuasive techniques, and other stylistic tools. In short, the Opposing Viewpoints Series is an ideal way to attain the higher-level thinking and reading skills so essential in a culture of diverse and contradictory opinions.

In addition to providing a tool for critical thinking, Opposing Viewpoints books challenge readers to question their own strongly held opinions and assumptions. Most people form their opinions on the basis of upbringing, peer pressure, and personal, cultural, or professional bias. By reading carefully balanced opposing views, readers must directly confront new ideas as well as the opinions of those with whom they disagree. This is not to argue simplistically that everyone who reads opposing views will—or should—change his or her opinion. Instead, the series enhances readers' understanding of their own views by encouraging confrontation with opposing ideas. Careful examination of others' views can lead to the readers' understanding of the logical inconsistencies in their own opinions, perspective on why they hold an opinion, and the consideration of the possibility that their opinion requires further evaluation.

Evaluating Other Opinions

To ensure that this type of examination occurs, Opposing Viewpoints books present all types of opinions. Prominent spokespeople on different sides of each issue as well as well-known professionals from many disciplines challenge the reader. An additional goal of the series is to provide a forum for other, less known, or even unpopular viewpoints. The opinion of an ordinary person who has had to make the decision to cut off life support from a terminally ill relative, for example, may be just as valuable and provide just as much insight as a medical ethicist's professional opinion. The editors have two additional purposes in including these less known views. One, the editors encourage readers to respect others' opinions—even when not enhanced by professional credibility. It is only by reading or listening to and objectively evaluating others' ideas that one can determine whether they are worthy of consideration. Two, the inclusion of such viewpoints encourages the important critical thinking skill of objectively evaluating an author's credentials and bias. This evaluation will illuminate an author's reasons for taking a particular stance on an issue and will aid in readers' evaluation of the author's ideas.

It is our hope that these books will give readers a deeper understanding of the issues debated and an appreciation of the complexity of even seemingly simple issues when good and honest people disagree. This awareness is particularly important in a democratic society such as ours in which people enter into public debate to determine the common good. Those with whom one disagrees should not be regarded as enemies but rather as people whose views deserve careful examination and may shed light on one's own.

Thomas Jefferson once said that "difference of opinion leads to inquiry, and inquiry to truth." Jefferson, a broadly educated man, argued that "if a nation expects to be ignorant and free . . . it expects what never was and never will be." As individuals and as a nation, it is imperative that we consider the opinions of others and examine them with skill and discernment. The Opposing Viewpoints series is intended to help readers achieve this goal.

David L. Bender and Bruno Leone,
Founders

Introduction

> *"Fifty years after the creation of NASA, our goal is no longer just a destination to reach. Our goal is the capacity for people to work and learn, and operate and live safely beyond the Earth for extended periods of time, ultimately in ways that are more sustainable and even indefinite. And in fulfilling this task, we will not only extend humanity's reach in space—we will strengthen America's leadership here on Earth."*
>
> —*Barack Obama*

After World War II, the United States and the Soviet Union became engaged in the Cold War, an era of intense political, ideological, economic, scientific, and social competition and conflict between the two global superpowers that would last until the downfall of the Soviet Union in 1991. Vital to America's security was a strong national defense, and the US government was determined to exploit the possibilities of space to protect the country and leverage any military or scientific advantage. In the late 1940s, the Department of Defense formulated a plan to orbit a satellite around Earth to gather scientific data. The Soviet Union countered by announcing their own plans to launch a satellite. The Soviets got theirs, called *Sputnik 1*, into space first on October 4, 1957.

The success of *Sputnik 1* galvanized public attention on the possibility of space exploration. Americans were concerned that a technological gap existed between the two countries—and that the Soviet Union was surging ahead of the United States in space. Worried that Soviet dominance would threaten national security, politicians and policy makers began to allocate the necessary resources to truly compete with the Soviets. Central to US success was the creation of a new agency, the National Aeronautics and Space Administration (NASA), which was established on October 1, 1958. NASA would be responsible for developing and directing US space programs and making sure America was a world leader in space exploration.

The United States launched its first Earth satellite, *Explorer 1*, on January 31, 1958. The satellite documented the existence of radiation zones encircling Earth. The promise of scientific discovery from space exploration thrilled scientists, policy makers, and the general public. As President Dwight D. Eisenhower noted in March 1958,

> [There are] many aspects of space and space technology . . . which can be helpful to all people as the United States proceeds with its peaceful program in space science and exploration. Every person has the opportunity to share through understanding in the adventures which lie ahead. This statement [of the President's Science Advisory Committee] makes clear the opportunities which a developing space technology can provide to extend man's knowledge of the earth, the solar system, and the universe. These opportunities reinforce my conviction that we and other nations have a great responsibility to promote the peaceful use of space and to utilize the new knowledge obtainable from space science and technology for the benefit of all mankind.

NASA quickly got to work advancing American interests in space. One of the agency's first programs involved the viability of human spaceflight, called Project Mercury. On May 5, 1961, Alan B. Shepard Jr. became the first American to fly into space; although he didn't orbit the Earth, he did successfully accomplish a suborbital mission. On April 12, 1961, the Soviets surged ahead of the United States again when Soviet cosmonaut Yuri Gagarin became the first man to orbit Earth in his Vostok spacecraft. On February 2, 1962, an American, John Glenn, became the second man to achieve orbit around Earth.

By the early 1960s, both the Soviets and Americans were feverishly planning to land a man on the moon. Project Gemini was vital to that effort; its ten spaceflights gathered much-needed information on weightlessness, reentry and splashdown procedures, spacecraft design and technology, and the rigors of spaceflight for human beings. One of the highlights of the Gemini program was the first spacewalk, which was done by astronaut Edward White on June 3, 1965.

The next major NASA program, Project Apollo, was created to take Americans to the moon. On July 20, 1969, astronauts Neil Armstrong and Edwin "Buzz" Aldrin were the first astronauts to land and walk on the moon's surface. At least five hundred million television viewers around the world watched the live coverage of the first moonwalk. The Apollo project cemented America's leadership in space and inspired scientists and space enthusiasts in every corner of the globe.

Before the moon landing even happened, however, NASA was already preparing for its next scientific and technological challenge: the space shuttle. Officially called the Space Transportation System (STS), the space shuttle is a winged, reusable orbiter designed to transport people and supplies and perform vital tasks, like conducting manned scientific experiments in orbit, servicing aging satellites and the Hubble Telescope, and carrying satellites into space. The first space shuttle, the *Columbia*, was launched on April 12, 1981, marking an exciting day in NASA history.

The space shuttle program also suffered a few heartbreaking tragedies. On January 28, 1986, the *Challenger* broke up shortly after takeoff, killing all seven crew members. It was later found that the accident was due to a faulty O-ring, a part used to seal off the solid-fuel rocket booster. On February 1, 2003, the *Columbia* broke apart on its reentry into

Earth's atmosphere, killing all seven astronauts aboard. Investigations of the accident showed that a piece of foam insulation had broken off during the launch and damaged the shuttle's thermal protection system. On July 21, 2011, the space shuttle program ended with the last flight of the *Atlantis*.

In 1990, the space shuttle *Discovery* launched the Hubble Space Telescope into orbit. The Hubble sent back awe-inspiring images of Earth and the rest of the universe and has provided observations that have led to breakthroughs in the field of astrophysics. Launched on November 7, 1996, the Mars global surveyor has been orbiting and sending back information on Mars since 1998. The Mars Pathfinder spacecraft landed on Mars on July 4, 1997, and explored the surface of the planet with its miniature rover, *Sojourner*.

In 2004, President George W. Bush announced his Vision for Space Exploration, which detailed NASA's new project: Project Constellation, made up of two launch vehicles and the Orion spacecraft. The Constellation program would take over the shuttle duties and have more capabilities than the shuttle. NASA would also push toward a manned spaceflight to Mars by 2020.

In 2010, however, President Barack Obama proposed a revised vision for NASA. Controversially, the plan called for the cancellation of Project Constellation, which he noted was over budget and behind schedule. Instead, he proposed using the money to pay commercial transport systems to do the work once done by the space shuttle. Many critics of the plan deride the idea of greater private sector involvement in space travel, arguing that the Obama administration is ceding US preeminence in space transportation to private companies.

In a 2010 speech at the Kennedy Space Center, Obama underscored the shifting priorities of the US space program and the need for a new vision for NASA. "The challenges facing our space program are different, and our imperatives for this program are different, than in decades past," he asserted. "We're no longer racing against an adversary. We're no longer competing to achieve a singular goal like reaching the Moon. In fact, what was once a global competition has long since become a global collaboration. But while the measure of our achievements has changed a great deal over the past 50 years, what we do—or fail to do—in seeking new frontiers is no less consequential for our future in space and here on Earth."

The authors of the viewpoints presented in *Opposing Viewpoints: NASA* explore competing visions for NASA's future and the US space program in the following chapters: What Should Be the Future of the NASA Space Program?, What Issues Surround the Space Shuttle Program?, How Should NASA Be Funded?, and What Role Should NASA Play in Diplomatic and Scientific Affairs? The information provided in this volume should offer insight into some of the challenges faced by NASA and controversies over its role in the twenty-first century.

OPPOSING VIEWPOINTS® SERIES

CHAPTER 1

What Should Be the Future of the NASA Space Program?

Chapter Preface

The future of human spaceflight, also known as manned spaceflight, has become an issue of some controversy in recent years. For many scientists and policy makers, human spaceflight is obsolete; technology has advanced to the point that most NASA missions can and should be performed by robots to avoid putting human beings in danger. Tragedies like the *Challenger* and *Columbia* shuttle disasters remind us that there is a real cost to launching people into space to repair a remote satellite or conduct scientific experiments. For many people, however, human spaceflight reflects the curiosity, courage, and rugged individualism of the human spirit and serves as an indicator of a nation's status and national strength. There is a reason why the Chinese are planning a manned spaceflight to the moon—it cements its first-class status as a nation with the resources and will to accomplish a very difficult goal. For China, it means joining an ultra-exclusive club of the most scientifically advanced and adventurous nations on Earth.

This emphasis on the importance of human spaceflight has its roots in the Cold War space race. As the United States and the Soviet Union faced off as ideological, economic, and political rivals, they also vied to be the first country to launch human beings into orbit around Earth. This contest was also regarded as vital for national security. On April 12, 1961, Soviet cosmonaut Yuri Gagarin took the honor of being the first man in space when he orbited Earth in his Vostok spacecraft. On February 2, 1962, an American, John Glenn, became the second man to achieve orbit around Earth.

It had become clear that the next big goal for human spaceflight would be the moon. In what became known as the Moon Race, both the Soviet Union and the United States directed all of their efforts to become the first country to successfully send human beings to the moon. When discussing US ambitions in space in 1962, President John F. Kennedy maintained, "We choose to go to the moon in this decade and do the other things, not because they are easy, but because they are hard, because that goal will serve to organize and measure the best of our energies and skills, because that challenge is one that we are willing to accept, one we are unwilling to postpone, and one which we intend to win, and the others, too."

On July 20, 1969, the United States won the Moon Race when the Apollo 11 spacecraft doors opened to allow astronauts Neil Armstrong and Edwin "Buzz" Aldrin to step onto the moon's surface. The feat thrilled Americans as well as people all over the world. At least five hundred million television viewers watched the live coverage of the first moonwalk. In subsequent Apollo missions, twelve Americans got the privilege of walking on the moon before the last manned lunar spaceflight, Apollo 17, in 1972.

Since that awe-inspiring moment, a number of men and women have taken manned spaceflights for various reasons. These highly trained and motivated individuals have ridden in the space shuttle; lived on the International Space Station; repaired remote space satellites and the Hubble Telescope; conducted scientific experiments and collected data; and paid large fees to participate in the emerging industry of space tourism. As a 2008 Massachusetts Institute of Technology report on the topic of human spaceflight concluded, "Human spaceflight has been the great human and technological adventure of the past half century. By putting people into places and situations unprecedented in history, it has stirred the imagination while expanding and redefining human experience."

Yet with the thrill and accomplishment of manned spaceflight comes the terrible risk. High-profile tragedies like the *Challenger* and *Columbia* shuttle disasters cost the lives of fourteen impressive men and women. A loss of life that profound often leads to a questioning of the ultimate need for and wisdom of human spaceflight in an age when technology allows us to perform the missions without the risk of loss of life.

The following chapter, which examines the future of the US space program, touches on the debate over human spaceflight. Other viewpoints in the chapter explore the government's vision for NASA, the goal of humans landing on Mars, and the establishment of a permanent settlement on the moon.

Viewpoint 1

> *"We need a program to reimagine a frontier that will allow us to open up this hunkered-down existence."*

The United States Needs a Robust Space Program

Bob Deutsch

Bob Deutsch is a cognitive anthropologist and founder of the firm Brain Sells, a strategic branding and communications consultancy. In the following viewpoint, he maintains that the United States needs a robust space program to counteract the national anxiety and malaise that has gripped the country for the past few years. Deutsch acknowledges that the space program is too expensive and will show few immediate benefits but argues that it fulfills the need to explore, learn, and conquer, which is a key component of the American psyche. He argues that at this crucial transitional moment in American history, the country must embrace the challenge of space exploration and remain open, creative, and curious if it is to remain at the forefront of global progress and leadership.

As you read, consider the following questions:

1. According to Deutsch, what do preliterate tribes have today that America does not have?

2. According to the author, what does creativity call for?
3. On what was the United States founded, according to Deutsch?

Before compromise budgetary legislation was passed earlier this fall [in 2010], Pres. Barack Obama had called for grounding NASA's space program that would have taken astronauts back to the moon and beyond. In seeking cheaper, faster ways of keeping the U.S. in an exploratory orbit, budgetary issues should not be the only consideration. The country needs a robust space program if we are to realize fully our psychic potential as explorer and player in an ever-expanding frontier.

Our nation finds itself on a treadmill, moving in a simple, two-dimensional motion, burning calories but not exactly sure where it is going. What is required for our national health is a balanced complexity of motion (and its attendant experience) that allows one to feel simultaneously "here" at the center and "out there" at the boundaries. Now, more than ever, in the midst of an economic downturn, and facing a future felt to be receding, Americans need to exist on two planes: the mundane and the mythic.

The Idea of America

Our Founding Fathers established the U.S. as an idea, not an ideal. The idea was of liberty and creativity combined, never to be constrained by the status quo. The vision of George Washington, Thomas Jefferson, Benjamin Franklin, and their band of brothers was rooted in the pragmatics of daily life and cast beyond the pale, into the boundless frontier.

The early 21st century certainly is a different time than the late 18th but, underneath the momentary talk, Americans maintain a deep appreciation and need for what this country represents. For instance, in the mid 1990s, I was talking to citizens concerning the proposed luxury car tariff against

Japanese automakers, a hot topic at the time. In one discussion, a young woman, a native of Detroit, said, "For a couple of generations, members of my family have worked here in the American auto industry. I'm scared about the Japanese competition, but I think tariffs are a bad idea." I asked her why. Upon hearing her response, the earth seemed to shake under the feet of the 11 people in that room, including me. She uttered just three short, but profound, sentences: "America is a good idea. The idea is freedom. Tariffs are a bad idea." The U.S.'s intrinsic nature is to be open and exploratory. That particularly is a good idea now. Curtailing the space program is a bad idea.

Liberty and Creativity

The thinking of this one woman reflects the essence of the relationship that liberty has to creativity—breaking out of routine and expected patterns and going beyond a top-of-mind, business-as-usual, short-term horizon. What is required to live in this frame of mind is having an idea of yourself as one who stands above the press of the moment. Such a mind-set allows a practical rootedness in one's authenticity and a "thinking up" that is optimistic and innovative. However, many Americans today feel boxed in by fear. Since words like "ponzi" and "derivatives" have entered their lexicon, they have been living in a question mark—heads down and shoulders hunched in a protective posture.

This is exactly why the U.S. must explore space. We need a program to reimagine a frontier that will allow us to open up this hunkered-down existence. The arguments against it are coldly logical and sometimes all too true. It is too expensive; there is little immediate benefit. The problem with those contentions is that they are blind to the human need to address the cosmic questions of life: Who are we? How are we unique? Why are we here? How did it all begin?

The U.S. has been a place—and should remain one—in which these types of questions are asked. Admittedly, these "big" questions may never be answered satisfactorily but, during the search, exploration itself becomes the driving force—our nation in search of the frontier, spatially and experientially. To make this happen, we need a sense of place that includes what is known and what is not, what is possible and what lies beyond our capabilities. Without such urgency of mind, the time frame of our intentions becomes shorter and our motives smaller-minded.

Rediscovering America's Mythology

As an anthropologist who traded his backpack and quinine tablets for a Hartmann two-suiter and Dramamine, I have lived among preliterate tribes who have no information technologies, malls, nor media. Their world falls far short of Utopia. Life is hard in the primeval forest, but what these weathered-skinned people do have is a general comfort level borne out of an assumed connectedness to their cosmos. Their mythology is rock-solid and enables them to carry on. The U.S. now finds itself "between mythologies." We are not what we once were (mostly because the world changed on us), and we do not yet know what we will become. Where once we had enough resources and weight to overcome any obstacle, we now face a world full of perplexing challenges. Space exploration can help the nation renew its national mythology.

How the country acts during this stage of identity transition will define what it becomes at the conclusion of this national *rite de passage*. To again take its place as a leader among nations and a beacon for all, the U.S. must remain open, imaginative, and creative; on the intellectual offense; and always exploring. It cannot succumb to the moment's impulse to recoil or resist. Space exploration provides a higher point of view from which to see ourselves. Such a vantage point paves the way for an openness of mind and a generosity of spirit.

We must go beyond metrics and groupthink. Data points are not people. Spreadsheets are not artful. To do something artfully requires a dynamic mix of imagination and understanding to see how the world might work. This is not a matter of being correct, but of provoking a self-referring reverie in people that elicits an expanded idea of themselves and their place in the world. As a result, they see anew.

This approach, of course, runs counter to today's government and corporate metric-mania that produces a diminished capacity to conceive bold and innovative visions and strategies. Numbers, budgetary or otherwise, can provide a means for measurement, but cannot "embody" or suggest meaningful insights into the human experience. Yet, such insights are the base coin of national and commercial success.

Unleashing Our National Creativity

Creativity calls for a focused subjectivity and the capacity to doubt: an ability to focus on something long enough and deep enough to conjure possibilities not seen in the manifest and immediate moment, along with a healthy acknowledgement that not everything is known. The unknown is fertile soil from which a world of wonders can be cultivated. Here, the plodding of facts and data is circumvented in a nonlinear, symbolic, not wholly rational way. In this maneuver, the mind plays a cognitive trick on itself by creating metaphor. "I will call what I do not know by the name of something that I do know." Suddenly, you become free to explore conceptually. You are released from the rut of the "now" and the already-known. Through this mental leapfrog, the creative impulse extrapolates into unknown scenarios. It moves from the past to instigate an inkling that lays the basis for the beginning of a new narrative, to a springboard that weaves a web of new patterns and associations, to an insinuation of the future as projected in metaphor. This process produces, from the outside-objective

The Value of the US Space Program

I know that some Americans have asked a question that's particularly apt on Tax Day: Why spend money on NASA at all? Why spend money solving problems in space when we don't lack for problems to solve here on the ground? And obviously our country is still reeling from the worst economic turmoil we've known in generations. We have massive structural deficits that have to be closed in the coming years.

But you and I know this is a false choice. We have to fix our economy. We need to close our deficits. But for pennies on the dollar, the space program has fueled jobs and entire industries. For pennies on the dollar, the space program has improved our lives, advanced our society, strengthened our economy, and inspired generations of Americans. And I have no doubt that NASA can continue to fulfill this role. (Applause.) But that is why—but I want to say clearly to those of you who work for NASA, but to the entire community that has been so supportive of the space program in this area: That is exactly why it's so essential that we pursue a new course and that we revitalize NASA and its mission—not just with dollars, but with clear aims and a larger purpose.

Barack Obama, Remarks by the President on Space Exploration in the 21st Century, John F. Kennedy Space Center, April 15, 2010. www.nasa.gov.

point of view, what can be perceived as seemingly off-topic meanderings, but nothing is further from the truth.

What is in operation is a kind of playfulness with ideas that is essential for creativity. This toying around contains a bunch of no's, as in no pretense, analyzing (yet), doubts, pressure to conform, restrictions, and, perhaps most important of all, judgment. Those who are playfully creative possess a curiosity given backbone by their expectation that they will find what they seek even though they do not know what it is they seek (often a statement of fact in space exploration).

In this special state of mental weightlessness, all inhabitants are joined by a belief in a beautiful human quality, directed serendipity: I have a plan because the plan allows me to begin to move forward and, in doing so, I learn about myself. You sort of go down a path and things evolve. By adapting and adjusting to randomness, you shape, but do not control, your endpoint. Yet, you define your endpoint by your own reaction to it—ah, ha! I like this. This is for me. This is me.

US Needs the Space Program

However, in sharp contrast, many more Americans today are losing hope in the ties that bind hard work to success. Many see the future as "closing." This mentality foreshortens their vision of self, others, and the world. This orientation, about almost everything, is defensive. Listen to the tone: money makes the world go around; now I have less money and hope—or, I feel better when I see someone worse off than me; I have to fight for everything, and I don't have a lot. In other words, what's the point?

The U.S. was founded on the idea of never accepting the status quo and always exploring further. It is our national heritage, and it is not nice to fool with a nation's nature. NASA's manned space program, particularly in times of uncertainty and fear, can help remind each American what it means to look up and open up—to have an idea of "you" that has a little elbow room.

Only the space program can provide a national effervescence that can give people that boost necessary to investigate their own essence, to write their own story. Manned exploration of space instigates a reverie to help people feel they are more fully alive and participating in a quest beyond the mundane. The very idea of breaking past Earth's pull can help keep people from being inundated by the contingency of any moment.

When thinking about one's own life, there is a sense of freedom in keeping the mind's eye oriented to the "out there, beyond the boundaries" of daily existence. To hold dear this attitude, it helps to realize that astronauts, space stations, the Hubble Telescope, etc. represent—and are a reflection of—who we are. More than any other idea, the NASA program allows people to experience the reality that we are but a small speck amidst the immensity of intergalactic space and that we are one with it. To partake daily of this mystery, to wonder, to feel and never flatline emotionally, lies at the core of the idea of manned space exploration. It is there to help each American—in the context of his or her own life—soar and explore.

Viewpoint 2

"Everyone has liked having a spaceflight program—but not enough to spend the kind of money required to sustain an endeavor as expensive, complex and dangerous as pushing humans beyond the atmosphere."

Grounding an American Dream

Keith Perine

Keith Perine is a writer for CQ. *In the following viewpoint, he points out that for years the US space program has been laboring under a policy of benign neglect and buffeted by budgetary fights, competing political priorities, and high-profile catastrophes. Perine explains that although Americans love the idea of a robust space program, they are ambivalent about spending the money on it. He predicts that national security concerns and national pride will insulate the space program from outright elimination, but tough economic times will lead it to languish at the bottom of national economic priorities.*

Keith Perine, "Grounding an American Dream," Congress.org, April 25, 2011. CQ.com.

As you read, consider the following questions:

1. According to the author, how much is the NASA budget in relationship to the total federal budget since the 1970s?
2. What effect did the 1986 *Challenger* tragedy have on the space program, according to Perine?
3. According to a 2010 CNN poll, what percentage of Americans said the money spent on the space shuttle would have been better spent on other things?

Government programs rarely die. But they do fade away. Look no further than NASA's human spaceflight venture, a perennially underfunded enterprise noteworthy for being high up on public opinion survey lists of optional government expenditures for years.

Nobody's ready to declare that the U.S. manned spaceflight program is over for good. But it's about to take a break that could last for years.

The scheduled April 29 launch of the space shuttle *Endeavour* is the next-to-last voyage for the aging shuttle fleet.

The final flight, of the *Atlantis* orbiter, is planned for June. While NASA supporters in Congress are pushing hard for a replacement vehicle and have engaged the Obama administration in what promises to be a long argument over NASA, no one knows when a NASA astronaut will leave Earth again on an American spacecraft.

This fadeaway took its own sweet time—more than three decades. Indeed, even as the public watched in wonder as the first shuttle shook the earth, lifted off and reached orbit exactly 30 years ago this month, policy makers were questioning the basic purpose, the value and especially the cost of the human spaceflight program.

The old doubts did not sideline the program. Instead, it suffered from benign neglect at the hands of Republican and

Democratic presidents and Congresses alike, as well as the public. But, now, while the program may be fading, the fights over it will not, as members of Congress cling to shuttle-related projects in their districts, and as politicians continue to see manned spaceflight as a source of national pride and economic competitiveness.

Ever since the Apollo program ended almost 40 years ago, NASA's spaceflight efforts have been hamstrung by tight budgets, buffeted by competing political priorities and twice marred by catastrophes from which the agency took years to recover.

The agency's budget has been fading away, too. It peaked in the mid-1960s, when it constituted about 4 percent of the overall federal budget. But it fell quickly after that, and it has hovered at around 1 percent of the total budget since the mid-1970s.

Everyone has liked having a spaceflight program—but not enough to spend the kind of money required to sustain an endeavor as expensive, complex and dangerous as pushing humans beyond the atmosphere.

"It's not dear enough to us to open the public treasury to the tune of about 5 percent of the federal budget," says Roger Launius, a curator at the Smithsonian Institution's National Air and Space Museum.

"Everybody thinks space is a good thing to do, but it's expendable in tough economic times," says Joan Johnson-Freese, a national security professor at the Naval War College.

For more than a year, President Obama and Congress have been at odds over the future direction of the spaceflight program.

Last year, Obama proposed what he considers a less expensive alternative, a wholesale shift away from government-run spaceflight toward a privatized system. Rather than paying for costly facilities to maintain costly equipment, the agency would simply be a customer, paying for seats and cargo bays on privately maintained spacecraft to fly to the International Space Station.

He proposed canceling the Constellation program, the agency's effort to develop follow-on spacecraft for the shuttles, saying in a speech at the Kennedy Space Center last year that this was the best way of ensuring that NASA could invest in new technologies with an eye toward launching ambitious exploration missions.

The administration sees a future in space too. It has set the goal of launching human spaceflight missions beyond the moon by 2025—perhaps to an asteroid—and sending astronauts to orbit Mars by the mid-2030s. But it's not clear how or when those goals will be met.

NASA's strongest supporters in Congress, many of them from states that stand to lose jobs from Obama's approach, pushed back hard to keep NASA in the human spaceflight business.

At a House committee hearing a few weeks after Obama submitted his proposal, Rep. Gabrielle Giffords, then chairwoman of the science subcommittee that oversees NASA, called the president's plans "a decimation of the most exciting project or program that the United States does." Giffords, an Arizona Democrat who was critically wounded in an assassination attempt in January, is married to NASA astronaut Mark Kelly, who will command the *Endeavour* mission.

NASA's allies made sure that most of the funds included in the agency's fiscal 2011 budget for space exploration will go toward NASA's continued development of a new rocket and capsule for human flight. But earlier this year, the agency said a similar amount in a 2010 NASA authorization bill wasn't enough.

To be sure, NASA does other things besides human spaceflight. Its satellites study the planet, and its telescopes and unmanned spacecraft peer far into the galaxy. But the manned spaceflight program has accounted for a big part of the agency's budget, and it is what has captivated congressional backers and the public for decades.

"Nobody throws a parade for robots," says Johnson-Freese.

The Apollo program, which put men on the moon, concluded the first act in manned spaceflight. But "there hasn't been a second act for space," says Howard McCurdy, an American University professor with an expertise in space policy. "It's been a one-act play so far."

The Apollo mission had a very different tenor than any other NASA spaceflight effort.

The order to go to the moon came from President John F. Kennedy. It was clear and specific in its goals, although its purposes were many and included beating the Russians at the height of the Cold War and making the young president look bold and daring.

"The reality is the Apollo program was part of a broad-based mobilization effort in the United States to best the Soviet Union in the Cold War," Launius says. "It was viewed as war by other means, in the same way foreign aid was viewed as war by other means."

The men who undertook the Apollo missions were anything but robots. They were folk heroes whose names fell from Americans' lips with the sort of ease that is now afforded only to movie stars and professional athletes.

It's impossible to know whether NASA would actually have met Kennedy's goal if he had lived. As it was, after Kennedy's assassination in Dallas, the lunar program was enshrined as his legacy.

"The reason we did Apollo was because Kennedy decided it was in the country's interest," said John Logsdon, a George Washington University professor. "And once he was killed, it became a memorial to him and basically untouchable."

Spurred by Kennedy's vision, Congress invested heavily in NASA's Apollo program. The agency was given a clearly defined goal, and the resources to match. In fact, it was the only time in which NASA's spaceflight vision and its budget have aligned, the only time that the agency didn't have to make decisions based on how much money it could wring out of Congress.

But it's one thing to aspire to the heavens, another to reach that goal—and yet another thing altogether to actually shell out the money to stay there. After collecting 842 pounds of moon rock samples in several missions from 1969 to 1972, the Apollo program ended in 1972.

"After Apollo it's just this shoestring, keep-things-moving kind of approach. There's no long-term strategy, because the strategic purpose was gone," Johnson-Freese says.

When the world was watching grainy images of Neil Armstrong and Buzz Aldrin walking on the moon in 1969, it would have been hard for anyone glued to a black-and-white television set to imagine that by 2011 the space agency would not have sent astronauts any farther into the solar system. And the notion that, four decades later, NASA would lose the ability to put humans into space at all would have been dismissed as laughable.

NASA had hoped to follow Apollo with an ambitious program of exploration and colonization. The agency envisioned space stations in orbit around Earth and the moon and on the lunar surface. As part of those overall plans, NASA proposed building a reusable space vehicle to ferry astronauts and cargo into space.

The proposal got scant attention from Kennedy's successor, Lyndon B. Johnson, who was embroiled in the Vietnam War and contentious domestic politics. After he succeeded Johnson, Richard Nixon showed little appetite for another costly, Kennedyesque space endeavor.

But the Cold War was still on, and it would have been politically unpalatable for Nixon to cede manned spaceflight to the Russians altogether, on the heels of the Apollo triumph. So at the beginning of 1972, Nixon signed off on the shuttle.

NASA had projected the cost of a reusable launcher and orbiter at $14 billion. Lawmakers balked at that price tag. So did Nixon's Office of Management and Budget, which told NASA it would have to make do with $5.5 billion. That meant design changes, including two solid rocket boosters and an external fuel tank.

To help sell the Nixon administration and Congress on the shuttle, NASA pitched the idea of a fleet that would travel to space frequently—as many as five launches a month by the early 1990s. The shuttle was positioned as America's only way to get either astronauts or payloads, including military ones, into space.

The constrained budget and NASA's ambitious plans for the shuttle forced the agency to make design decisions, partly to satisfy the military's need for a "cross-range" craft that could fly east or west after reentering the atmosphere.

"As advertised in 1972, the shuttle was going to be routine, inexpensive and safe," Logsdon said. "And it was none of those three."

Still, for the first few years of shuttle flights, NASA tried to portray them as routine. Democratic Sen. Bill Nelson of Florida traveled aboard *Columbia* in early 1986.

A couple of weeks later, schoolteacher Christa McAuliffe was part of the crew for a *Challenger* flight. NASA planned to send up a reporter on a subsequent voyage.

But those plans, and the entire shuttle program, changed when *Challenger* blew up 73 seconds after launch. Images of excited children in classrooms across America were replaced by images of the shuttle's destruction, replayed over and over on national television.

The shuttle drew unprecedented scrutiny as a result of the accident, including a televised hearing by an independent commission and a damning report about the culture at the agency that produced a wholesale shake-up.

But as Kennedy's death helped propel Apollo, the *Challenger* tragedy seemed to propel the shuttle.

As he mourned the death of the seven *Challenger* crew members, President Ronald Reagan felt the need to call for more, not fewer, shuttle flights. "Nothing ends here," he said. "Our hopes and our journeys continue."

The accident grounded the shuttle fleet for 32 months, and there was no more talk of teachers and reporters hitching rides. Before the shuttles started flying again, the Reagan administration decided that they also would no longer carry commercial satellites or military payloads.

And any romance attached to the shuttle fleet vanished on the cold winter morning when *Challenger* was destroyed.

The End of the Shuttle?

The real turning point for NASA came in 2003, when the *Columbia* orbiter disintegrated over the United States during reentry. A blue-ribbon commission that studied the catastrophe had little trouble identifying the cause: Superheated gases had entered a hole along the left wing caused by a piece of foam that had fallen off the external fuel tank during launch. But the board also drew another, equally damning conclusion: that the shuttle fleet to which NASA had devoted its spaceflight energies for 30 years should be replaced.

"Because of the risks inherent in the original design of the space shuttle, because that design was based on many aspects of now-obsolete technologies, and because the shuttle is now an aging system but still developmental in character, it is in the nation's interest to replace the shuttle as soon as possible as the primary means for transporting humans to and from Earth orbit," the board announced in its August 2003 report.

Budget woes infected plans for replacing the shuttle as well. President George W. Bush responded to the post-

Columbia commission's report in 2004 with an ambitious plan, dubbed the Vision for Space Exploration. Under it, the shuttle fleet would be retired by 2010, and NASA would go back to sending astronauts into space in crew capsules on top of rockets. Robots would go to the moon by 2008, and humans would go by 2020, in preparation for further missions to Mars and other destinations.

NASA attempted to fulfill Bush's vision with what became known as the Constellation program, including a set of rockets, a crew capsule and a lunar lander. But NASA's assumptions about program funding didn't match up with the money it got from Congress. Between the lack of funding and technical issues that arose in the design process, the deadlines for Constellation components slipped.

"The problem was that NASA, in the intervening years, was starved of money, and the new rocket wasn't ready for flight by the time the space shuttle was being shut down," said Nelson, who rode on the shuttle as a young congressman in 1986 and who is the spaceflight program's most prominent congressional defender.

During its three decades of flight, the shuttles revolutionized space travel. They were the first reusable spacecraft. NASA used them to launch satellites, launch and repair the massive Hubble Space Telescope, and build the International Space Station. In the early years of the shuttle fleet, the orbiters were used to conduct scientific experiments in several fields, including fluid physics and astronomy. They sometimes carried a portable space laboratory, Spacelab, that was developed with the European Space Agency. The shuttles were able not only to launch satellites and other spacecraft but to retrieve them as well.

Obama inherited a spaceflight program in disarray. He commissioned another blue-ribbon study, known as the Augustine commission after its chairman, former Lockheed Martin Corp. CEO Norman Augustine. In August 2009, six years after the *Columbia* accident report, the Augustine commission concluded that the Constellation program had "faced a mismatch between funding and program content" since it began.

The commission recommended a series of options for human spaceflight rather than any single path forward. But it also flatly concluded that space exploration beyond low Earth orbit wasn't possible under NASA's fiscal 2010 funding level, and that the agency needed $3 billion more per year if it was to conduct "meaningful human exploration."

Several months later, Obama roiled the space community with his fiscal 2011 budget proposal for NASA. The president proposed canceling Constellation and devoting substantially more money to funding independent efforts by the private sector. Obama also wanted to boost funding for technological research and development on things such as propulsion systems, to lay a new groundwork for future long-distance space exploration.

Obama's critics often accuse him of being too fond of government solutions to the nation's problems. But his fiscal 2011 budget proposal for NASA represented a wholesale shift away from government-run spaceflight to low Earth orbit and toward a privatized system.

Obama highlighted the shift in his April 2010 speech at the Kennedy Space Center. He also defended his decision to cancel Constellation as the best option for ensuring that NASA eventually could launch ambitious exploration missions with finite resources. He declared that he was "100 percent committed to the mission of NASA and its future." And Obama outlined his own lofty vision for future space travel.

"Our goal is the capacity for people to work and learn, operate and live safely beyond the Earth for extended periods of time, ultimately in ways that are more sustainable and even indefinite," Obama declared.

A new batch of companies has sprung up alongside the traditional NASA contractors to compete for "commercial crew" services. The leading such company, Space Exploration Technologies—SpaceX for short—was founded in 2002 by Internet entrepreneur Elon Musk. Last December, SpaceX became the first private company in history to launch a vehicle into low Earth orbit and recover it.

SpaceX and another company, Orbital Sciences Corp., already have contracts with NASA to fly cargo to the International Space Station after the shuttle fleet has retired.

But lawmakers aren't convinced that SpaceX and other prospective commercial carriers are going to be able to ferry astronauts safely within the next few years. They have defied Obama by forbidding the agency to get out of the rocket-building business altogether. That's too radical a departure from NASA's path for the agency's congressional backers to stomach.

Within several weeks after Obama's dramatic proposal last year, Nelson and his Senate allies forced the president to make a major concession: Although Constellation would be canceled, NASA would retain development of two of its key elements, a heavy-lift rocket for traveling beyond low Earth orbit and a crew capsule.

NASA pledged to find the money for the new rocket and capsule within the president's fiscal 2011 request. But lawmakers, particularly in the House, were skeptical.

"It does no good to cancel a program that the administration characterizes as 'unexecutable' if that program is simply replaced with a new plan that can't be executed either," said the chairman of the House Science and Technology Committee, Democrat Bart Gordon of Tennessee, at a May 2010 hearing.

Nelson and Texas Republican Kay Bailey Hutchison wrote a NASA authorization bill that codified Obama's concessions, with less money for crew efforts than the president had requested and nearly $3 billion for NASA's rocket and capsule efforts. Nelson also added an extra space shuttle flight to the space station, the *Atlantis* flight now planned for June.

Nelson and Hutchison pushed their bill through the Senate last August and persuaded reluctant House Democrats to clear it in September.

But even before it got its final fiscal 2011 appropriation figure, NASA issued a blunt warning in January that the funds authorized for the new rocket and capsule in Nelson's bill were not sufficient. "The cost and operational capability of the systems must be sustainable over multiple administrations and multiple Congresses," the agency told lawmakers. "Any designs selected also must meet the test of being realistic—not relying on assumptions of increased funding or other 'miracles' for attainment."

Nelson, Hutchison and their Senate allies fired back in a joint statement making it clear that they expected NASA to stay on track this time. "The production of a heavy-lift rocket and capsule is not optional. It's the law," the senators declared. "NASA must use its decades of space know-how and billions of dollars in previous investments to come up with a concept that works. We believe it can be done affordably and efficiently—and it must be a priority."

In the final fiscal 2011 spending bill, NASA got $18.5 billion—less than the $18.7 billion it received for fiscal 2010 and less than the $19 billion Obama had wanted. But in today's climate, that counts as emerging unscathed. Lawmakers allocated $3.8 billion for space exploration, but they specified that $3 billion of that was to be spent on NASA's new rocket and capsule.

NASA officials plan to deliver by June a final report to Congress about how it intends to develop that new equipment.

So human spaceflight—NASA style—remains in doubt now more than ever in the 50-year history of the space program. A critical question is: Do Americans care?

Historically, Americans have loved exploration and tales of exploration, real and fictional. Portrayals of humans on the moon preceded actual humans on the moon by at least a century, with Jules Verne's *From the Earth to the Moon.*

The fruits of the program—advances in science and engineering—are numerous. The air and space museum in Washington is among the most visited museums on the planet.

But support for the space program, while always intense and consistent among certain groups, has been shaky when money is tight, with polls showing that the space program is seen as a place to cut.

Launius points to old polling data showing that the level of public support for sending men to the moon held steady, around 40 percent, from 1961 to 1995. But, he notes, public opinion polls in the 1960s, during the height of the space race, showed that spaceflight was always near the top of the list of programs Americans would cut in favor of other priorities.

A CNN poll from last August showed that things haven't changed all that much: Forty-nine percent of respondents said the shuttle has been a worthwhile and important program, but 50 percent said the money would have been better spent on other things.

But that doesn't mean the public would necessarily go along with killing the spaceflight program outright.

"Saying we're not going to do this thing or we're no longer going to do this thing is stepping back from our great-nation status, and I don't think the public would go along," Launius says.

"I think public fascination with spaceflight has fallen off, but I think that is a natural process," says Michael Robinson, a history professor at the University of Hartford in Connecticut. Robinson said that during American exploration of the polar regions in 1850s, the first expeditions were "unbelievably popular, and the first explorers were superstars; they were celebrities as popular as Neil Armstrong. But over time, like anything, when you're exposed to anything over and over, you become kind of desensitized to it. So that interest falls off."

For as long as men have been going into space, we've been debating whether there's any real reason to send them there.

"I think you can only justify the cost of human spaceflight, particularly exploration to Mars, on the basis of expanding new frontiers, on the basis of non-quantitative, esoteric arguments," says Lockheed Martin's Augustine, adding, "Great nations take on great challenges, they do this kind of thing. But I don't think you build an economic argument for it."

Proponents also say NASA needs to keep its human spaceflight program so that the United States can keep being a leader in international space policy.

"I think that part of the urgency, if you will, is not a political race, but the fact that the world is developing and other people are going to be operating and working in space, and if we want to have influence over how the international rules develop and how relationships in this high-tech world develop, then we have to be there," says Scott Pace, director of George Washington University's Space Policy Institute.

But even though the public is halfhearted at best about the spaceflight program, it would be tough for lawmakers to end it completely. While the program has been allowed to languish, its bipartisan supporters in Congress feel more passionately about maintaining it than other lawmakers do about ending it.

The Cold War is over, but NASA's congressional backers still invoke the same kind of "us vs. them" argument, saying we can't simply abandon manned spaceflight and allow other nations' efforts, especially those of Russia and China, to proceed without us. "Space is America's military high ground," said Florida Republican Bill Posey.

Much as it has for the last 40 years, that argument, an equal mix of national security and national prestige, will insulate NASA's human spaceflight program from outright elimination. But a tough fiscal climate and a lack of sustained public interest in the program will leave the program where it has languished for decades: without a sustainable vision, and a shadow of its former self.

VIEWPOINT 3

> *"The United States should become a spacefaring nation, and the leader of a spacefaring civilization."*

NASA Needs a Clear Vision for Its Future

Rand Simberg

Rand Simberg is an aerospace engineer and a consultant in space commercialization, space tourism, and Internet security. In the following viewpoint, he argues that the American people must rethink the vision for NASA, focusing on what is economically feasible and profitable in the future. Simberg observes that NASA must not only explore space, but also find ways to develop it in cooperation with private interests that would have low marginal costs of operation. He contends that when NASA is able to unleash private enterprise and create jobs and wealth, it will reach its full potential.

As you read, consider the following questions:

1. According to Simberg, what did John Marburger say about the future of the space program?

Rand Simberg, "A Space Program for the Rest of Us," *The New Atlantis*, Summer 2009, pp. 3–4, 18–20, 25–27.

2. According to a recent Aerospace Corporation study, what is the total cost of the Ares I program?
3. Why does the author believe that the Missile Defense Agency made great progress?

Four decades have passed since the first small step on the dusty surface of our nearest neighbor in the solar system in 1969. It has been almost that long since the last man to walk on the Moon did so in late 1972. The Apollo missions were a stunning technological achievement and a significant Cold War victory for the United States. However, despite the hope of observers at the time—and despite the nostalgia and mythology that now cloud our memory—Apollo was not the first step into a grand human future in space. From the perspective of forty years, Apollo, for all its glory, can now be seen as a detour away from a sustainable human presence in space. By and large, the NASA programs that succeeded Apollo have kept us heading down that wrong path: Toward more bureaucracy. Toward higher costs. And away from innovation, from risk taking, and from any concept of space as a *useful* place.

The Curse of Success

In a sense, Apollo occurred too soon. Had you asked the boldest science fiction writers in, say, 1954 whether men would walk on the Moon within a decade and a half, they would have scoffed—and justifiably so. Even though writers of fiction and nonfiction alike had theorized for decades about putting objects into orbit, and even though work was already under way in 1954 to put the first small unmanned satellites into orbit, the notion that we could develop so rapidly the capability to put men on the Moon on a politically feasible budget would have seemed ludicrous.

Unforeseeable in 1954 were the historical contingencies that led to the Apollo program's conception: the panicked public reaction to *Sputnik* in the United States in 1957; the young and charismatic Cold War president [John F. Kennedy] who ran and won on the issue of a "missile gap" with the Soviet Union in 1960; the Soviets' success in putting the first man in orbit in the third month of the young presidency; and that president's humiliation at the Bay of Pigs. And who could have known that, just thirty months after announcing the goal "before this decade is out, of landing a man on the Moon and returning him safely to the Earth," the young president would be cut down—leaving the nation, and the next president, to meet the goal now consecrated to his memory?

The Fundamental Problem

In the blink of an eye, a subject purely in the realm of science fiction became science fact—and a major cultural phenomenon, not to mention a huge government program. At its funding peak during the Apollo years, NASA consumed over four percent of the entire federal budget. The funding would not have flowed so freely if not for the urgency of the race with the Soviets. Had the Soviets been rushing not up to space but down to the bottom of the Marianas Trench [the deepest part of the world's oceans] (which had in fact just been reached in 1960), the United States would have spent lavishly to get there first. Had Kennedy not been assassinated and had he won a second term, he might well have ended the Apollo program himself as it became clear that we were winning the space race and as the race became less urgent in the face of other national priorities. A couple of months before his death, Kennedy even told NASA administrator James Webb that he "wasn't that interested in space."

And that has been NASA's fundamental problem ever since. The American people and their representatives in Congress are just not that interested in space, and never have been, going all the way back to Apollo. And it shows in our space policy, which has from the start been confused and contradictory. . . .

Rethinking the Vision

To get past the misperceived lessons of the past four decades and to develop a "safe, innovative, affordable, and sustainable" plan for manned spaceflight, we must begin by stating plainly why we should go into space, for the *why* gives shape to the *how*.

The United States should become a spacefaring nation, and the leader of a spacefaring civilization.

That means that access to space should be almost as routine (if not quite as affordable) as access to the oceans, and with similar laws and regulations. It means thousands, or millions, of people in space—and not just handpicked government employees, but private citizens spending their own money for their own purposes. It means that we should have the capability to detect an asteroid or comet heading for Earth and to deflect it in a timely manner. Similarly it means we should be able to mine asteroids or comets for their resources, for use in space or on Earth, potentially opening up new wealth for the planet. It means that we should explore the solar system the way we did the West: not by sending off small teams of government explorers—Lewis and Clark were the extreme exception, not the rule—but by having lots of people wandering around and peering over the next rill in search of adventure or profit.

We should have massively parallel exploration—and not just exploration, but development, as it has worked on every previous frontier. We need to expand the economic sphere into the solar system, as John Marburger, George W. Bush's science adviser, used to say in his speeches. We need to think in terms of *wealth* creation, not just job creation. That would be "affordable and sustainable," almost by definition.

The Economic Perspective

You may say I'm a dreamer, but I'm not the only one: Apollo left many orphans. But it's not a dream shared by NASA, suc-

NASA Strategy Based on Long-Term Affordability

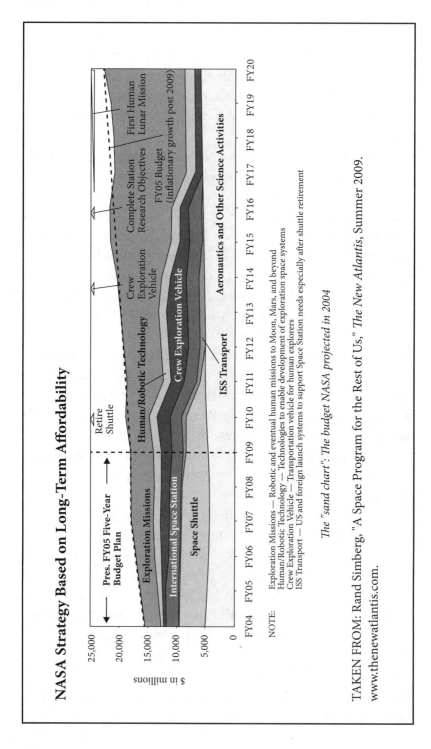

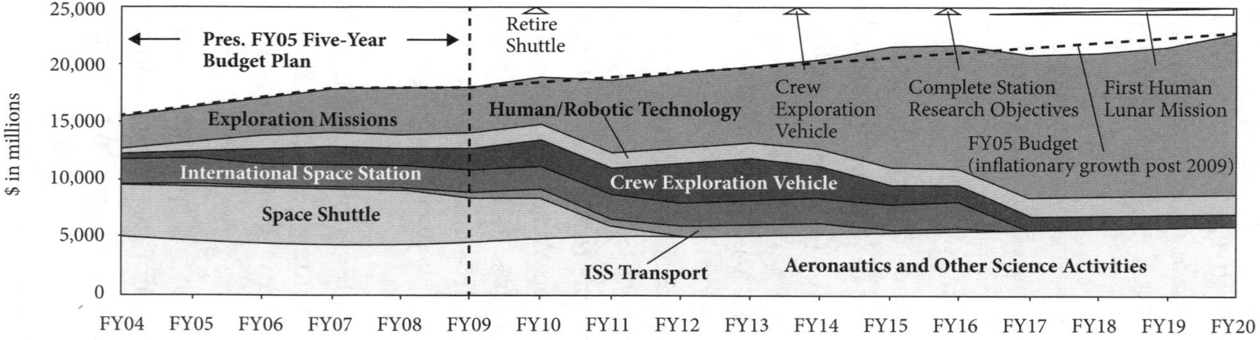

NOTE: Exploration Missions — Robotic and eventual human missions to Moon, Mars, and beyond
Human/Robotic Technology — Technologies to enable development of exploration space systems
Crew Exploration Vehicle — Transportation vehicle for human explorers
ISS Transport — US and foreign launch systems to support Space Station needs especially after shuttle retirement

The "sand chart": The budget NASA projected in 2004

TAKEN FROM: Rand Simberg, "A Space Program for the Rest of Us," *The New Atlantis*, Summer 2009. www.thenewatlantis.com.

cessive presidents, or members of Congress, at least to judge by their plans over the past four decades. We have had a monolithic government space agency for half a century at a cumulative cost of roughly half a trillion dollars (in current-year dollars). If we are going to continue to spend that order of magnitude of money—as, for political reasons, it seems we are going to do indefinitely—we should at least have something more to show for it than just a couple hundred brief trips to orbit for elite civil servants at an average cost over that period of about a couple billion dollars per flight. NASA needn't do all the work of making space affordable and sustainable, but it ought to do *something*. To put it another way, it isn't NASA's job to put humans on Mars; it's NASA's job to make it possible for the National Geographic Society, or an offshoot of the Latter-Day Saints, or an adventure tourism company, to put humans on Mars.

In concrete economic terms, that implies that whatever infrastructure we establish for reaching space should have low, not high, marginal costs of operation. Low marginal costs mean that as demand for a service grows, the price can drop rapidly. For example, a large restaurant with a full staff (a high fixed cost) but only a couple of diners would have to charge thousands of dollars each for a meal. But the marginal cost of feeding the next diner is only the cost of the food, and as the restaurant fills, the average cost can drop to where the price of a meal becomes affordable. (In this analogy our current spaceflight practices are akin to burning down all the restaurant's furniture after every meal and buying it all anew before the next one; marginal costs are quite high in that scenario.)

Addressing Economic Constraints

High marginal costs will forever constrain the level of activity that's possible. That was true of Apollo, it is true of what NASA currently plans with Constellation, and it is true of any

Constellation-like architecture (such as DIRECT): every flight will require throwing away tens if not hundreds of millions of dollars worth of hardware. If we were, say, to discover something on the Moon really worth going after, our ability to ramp up activity with Constellation would be severely limited by our budget. Low marginal costs provide *scalability*, which is essential for any technology that is going to open up large new markets. NASA's plans completely lack any understanding of this crucial principle.

The principle of low marginal (and average) costs was why the shuttle was created, except that it ended up combining the worst of all cost worlds: the shuttle has high fixed costs (for the standing army needed to service it), high average costs (resulting from the low flight rates), and high marginal costs (due to the hardware thrown away with each flight). When you hear that a space shuttle flight cost hundreds of millions of dollars, that figure is an average cost—the annual cost of the overall shuttle program divided by the number of flights that year (dividing the total cost of the shuttle program since its inception by the total number of flights would result in a yet higher number). The actual marginal cost (the cost of flying one more mission, given that you are already flying) is much lower, at most $150 million—still ridiculously high, but comparable to other launch vehicles with much less capability.

The Cost of the Constellation Program

How does Constellation stack up? Let's ignore the crew module Orion and just look at Ares I, the crew launch vehicle. A recent Aerospace Corporation study estimated that the total cost of the Ares I program—all the costs of the program from inception to grave—would be $19 billion for fourteen flights. This figure was obviously based on the initial development cost estimate of $14 billion; using the current estimated development costs of $35 billion, the total cost for Ares I would actually be about $40 billion. Even under the most charitable interpretation of the numbers—not including all the development costs and generously assuming four flights per year and fixed costs of just $1 billion per year—each Ares I flight would still cost roughly the same as each shuttle flight, although with much less capacity. And that figure doesn't include the Orion capsule, let alone the Ares V heavy-lift vehicle with all the expensive lunar mission hardware aboard. Each lunar mission, in this architecture, will cost several billion dollars.

Mike Griffin [the former NASA chief] was wont to compare Constellation to the U.S. Interstate Highway System. But the interstate was a national investment that resulted in a system with very low marginal costs and affordable for all. Anyone with a car could get on it, drive at high speeds, and just gas up when they got to a station. Its network of roads was also a boon to national security (which was in fact its initial justification). By contrast, Constellation (and any similar architecture) doesn't just fail to support national security (thereby ignoring one of the Aldridge commission recommendations). It is also a huge money sink that will result in a system with high marginal costs, low flight rates, and only for use by government employees. . . .

Recommendations for the Augustine Committee

Just as war is too important to be left to the generals, man's future in space is too important to be left to NASA. After President Reagan proposed the creation of a national missile defense system in 1983, it became clear that the U.S. Air Force was not properly organized or motivated—and so a new agency was created to pursue the president's vision. The new agency, today called the Missile Defense Agency, was very innovative and made great progress because it could focus on its one goal. Along those lines, the [George W.] Bush administration might have done well to establish an Office of Space Development (with "exploration" being merely a means to an end) that could draw on other federal resources—not just NASA, but the Departments of Defense and Energy—as well as the private sector.

Of course, an independent space development organization with such power would be politically unfeasible. But that is part of the problem: our sclerotic space agency is subject to forces of legacy politics; it protects existing bureaucratic structures and emphasizes jobs over achievement; and it perversely rewards failure with more funds and punishes success with budget cuts. Short of an independent entity, the Augustine committee [a 2009 commission tasked with reviewing US spaceflight plans] should at least revisit the Aldridge commission's recommendation of converting the NASA centers to FFRDCs [federally funded research and development centers].

Assuming, though, that NASA in roughly its present form is here to stay, what should the Augustine committee recommend to put the agency back on the right course?

Abandon New Launch System

First, there is great irony (as space blogger Clark Lindsey has noted) in the fact that NASA has not successfully developed a launch system in decades, with many failed attempts, whereas it has developed many techniques and technologies for orbital assembly and operations—and yet it is pouring billions of dollars into the former and neglecting the latter. Critics often bemoan NASA's abandonment of Saturn rocket technology upon the end of the Apollo era. But to abandon the orbital assembly and operations technology developed during the shuttle era—as the Constellation architecture implicitly does; it doesn't even call for an airlock on the new crew capsule for the crew to conduct extravehicular activities—would be a much greater tragedy, because unlike the Saturn infrastructure it actually offers a path to a future of abundant low-cost space activities.

The COTS Program

Donald Rumsfeld, the former Secretary of Defense, infamously remarked that "you go to war with the army you have." NASA should have planned on going to the Moon with the launch vehicles it had and not those it wanted to have; in retrospect, the agency should have been explicitly forbidden from developing a new launch system. Billions have already been wasted in developing a redundant launch capability when the focus should have been on getting beyond low Earth orbit. The space agency must finally, after half a century, be a good customer, and provide a market not for cost-plus contractors to build hardware at their direction, but for private transportation services. The Commercial Orbital Transportation Services (COTS) program should be revitalized with additional funding, new entrants should be invited, and its role should be broadened far beyond the current charter to service the International Space Station—to supporting exploration itself. In addition, COTS D (for delivery of crew to the International Space Station in addition to cargo) should be immediately funded, to provide redundant means of getting passengers to and from orbit and the space station on American hardware. A robust COTS program, in combination with a requirement that companies begin to deliver hundreds of tons of propellant into orbit each year, would provide enough traffic and competition among launch providers to finally start to drive down the cost of access to space. This would be a welcome change from the stagnation of high launch costs over the past few decades, and an improvement over the promise of still higher costs from Constellation. The aim should be to develop architectures that are not dependent on any particular launcher but that are redundant both in their ability to get to orbit and to travel between nodes beyond Earth.

Research and Technology

Third, the savings from avoiding the development of unnecessary new launch systems should be spent on resurrecting the

Research and Technology program initiated by Admiral [Craig E.] Steidle. Specifically, NASA should work on developing the tools and techniques needed to store and transfer cryogenic propellants in orbit. The agency should begin to define requirements for (redundant) propellant depots, and perform studies on optimal locations for such depots. NASA should perform experiments in propellant handling at the International Space Station, and it should lease space in a Bigelow [Aerospace] orbital habitat at low inclination as a test bed for orbital transportation support operations. The agency should do with its space transportation needs what the U.S. Postal Service did with its airmail needs back in the thirties: create a vibrant new transportation industry. And it should provide the kind of technology development support that NASA's predecessor, the old National Advisory Committee for Aeronautics, did for aviation in the first half of the twentieth century.

Let us finally abandon our race with the Soviet Union, the race we won four decades ago against an adversary two decades vanquished and vanished. We don't need to remake Apollo; we need to open up the new space frontier the way the old American frontier was opened. Let us unleash private enterprise and create not just jobs but true wealth. Let us innovate and find new ways for free men and women to use new resources. And let us work hard and risk greatly in the pursuit of our individual dreams—for it is those dreams, and our countless failures and triumphs along the way, that will determine man's destiny beyond the Earth.

VIEWPOINT 4

> *"For the foreseeable future space exploration will be undertaken mainly by machines that don't horrify a watching world when they die slowly, with no hope of rescue."*

Human Spaceflight Should End

Michael Lind

Michael Lind is an author, a columnist for Salon.com, and a policy director at the New America Foundation. In the following viewpoint, he applauds the transition to unmanned spaceflight, arguing that robot space probes have been so successful that there is no need to risk human lives for space exploration anymore. Lind also shoots down the idea of privately sponsored human spaceflight, pointing out that national security concerns will severely curtail the ability of private interests to fund human spaceflight in the future. In fact, he predicts that in the next few generations the only kind of human spaceflight will be on a small scale.

Michael Lind, "Why We Should Embrace the End of Human Spaceflight," Salon.com, April 12, 2011. This article first appeared in Salon.com, at http://www.salon.com. An online version remains in the Salon archives.

As you read, consider the following questions:

1. As explained by Lind, what American robot space vehicles have visited Mars in recent years?
2. How does the author respond to the assertion that humans look to transcend the boundaries of Earth?
3. What does Lind believe humans are likely to do if a natural catastrophe rendered the surface of Earth inhabitable?

This week [April 10–16, 2011] NASA is announcing where the soon-to-be-retired space shuttles will be displayed as museum relics. On April 19 the space shuttle *Endeavour* will be launched, on the penultimate mission of the program. The end of the space shuttle program will mean that the U.S. will have to rely on Russian rockets to deliver American astronauts to space, pending the development of private commercial spaceflight.

It is tempting to say that this is an outrage; that the effective end of the American manned spaceflight program is a national humiliation; that the program's demise is yet another symbol of the gap in mentality between the confident, ambitious Kennedy-Johnson years and today's solipsistic, penny-pinching America. It is tempting to say all that, but the temptation should be resisted.

The Success of the US Space Program

The truth is that the American space program is flourishing. In recent years Mars has been visited by the *Phoenix* [Mars] lander and the Mars rovers, *Spirit* and *Opportunity*. At the moment the MESSENGER [MErcury Surface, Space Environment, GEochemistry and Ranging] probe is orbiting Mercury and the New Horizons probe is scheduled to pass Pluto in 2015. With the help of the orbiting Kepler space telescope, more than 500 planets in other solar systems have been identified. We live in the greatest age of cosmic exploration in history, even if the public pays little attention because there are no astronauts to engage in white-knuckle landings or to clown around for the cameras.

When the Apollo astronauts landed on the moon, many assumed that this was the first step toward permanent colonization of the moon and journeys by astronauts to other planets. From today's perspective, though, the space race was like the races to the North Pole and the South Pole. Once explorers had reached those destinations, the world lost interest.

Another parallel is ocean exploration. Back in the 1960s, visions of colonies on the moon competed with plans for domed cities on the ocean floor that gave a new meaning to the phrase "real estate bubble." Scientific exploration of the ocean depths continues to produce marvelous discoveries, like whole ecosystems that have evolved to take advantage of the heat and emissions of undersea volcanic vents. But the year 2000 came and went and millions of homeowners are "underwater" only in metaphor.

The parallel is not complete, of course. The poles and the ocean depths are far more hospitable to human life than near Earth orbit or the moon or Mars. Astronauts have learned that prolonged weightlessness does terrible things to the bones and the circulatory system. If God wanted us to live in outer space, we wouldn't have balancing systems in our inner ears. When and if the science-fiction alternative of providing a simulacrum of gravity by spinning a spaceship or space station is tried, let us hope there will be a plentiful supply of barf bags.

Weak Arguments for Human Spaceflight

The worst enemies of human spaceflight are its proponents. Their arguments are so weak that you keep waiting for the real, knock-down argument, which never comes.

The success of robot space probes has discredited the idea that machines are too stupid to do science in space. When that argument for human spaceflight collapses, those that remain are preposterous.

One is the assertion that life has always sought out new environments. Just as plants and animals moved from the seas to the land, it is said, so humanity must transcend the boundaries of the Earth.

This is just silly. Animals never leave a comfortable habitat for a harsh one, unless they are forced to. That is why we don't see buffalo, raccoons and turtles marching off to Death Valley in great numbers to test their mettle, in a spirit of adventure.

Our vertebrate ancestors did not come ashore hundreds of millions of years ago because they decided to boldly go where no fish had gone before. Instead, generations of proto-amphibians in shallow water got stranded in separated ponds. The ones that were accidentally equipped to survive by desperately gulping air survived long enough to breed, and here we and our fellow land animals are. No lungfish congress would have voted to colonize dry land.

Equally silly is the comparison between the exploration of America by Europeans and the exploration of outer space. The Americas had native people to be enslaved by greedy Europeans, abundant resources and lots of pleasant places to live—to say nothing of breathable air and drinkable water. That's why the European powers fought to control the Western Hemisphere, while ignoring the continent of Antarctica.

Avoiding Extinction?

What about the argument that part of the human race needs to dwell somewhere other than on Earth, if humanity is to avoid extinction? In 500 million years the gradually warming sun may boil the oceans, and a few billion years later the sun will evolve into a red giant, incinerating or engulfing the Earth. Our descendants, if there are any, might consider relocating.

In the half-billion years until then, the chances of war, plague or global warming producing the total extinction of a species as numerous, widespread and versatile as humanity are pretty low. A sufficiently large asteroid or comet impact like the one that caused the extinction of the dinosaurs could do the job. But if a massive bolide threatened the Earth, we would send unmanned spacecraft, not [actors] Robert Duvall or Bruce Willis, to steer it away or destroy it.

In the event some other natural catastrophe—a supervolcano, a nearby supernova—rendered the surface of the Earth temporarily or permanently uninhabitable, it would be cheaper and easier to build and maintain underground bunkers than to use the same technology to do the same thing at vastly greater cost on the moon or other planets or in space stations. By the same token, if humanity had the technology to "terraform" the surface of Mars, it would have the power to make the ruined surface of a dead Earth habitable again, making the colonization of Mars unnecessary.

The Myth of Private Investment

If there is no compelling argument for government-sponsored human spaceflight, there is no convincing rationale for private commercial spaceflight, either. The Robert Heinlein [an American science-fiction author] wing of science-fiction fandom has always combined Tea Party–style anti-statism with a love of big rockets. Now that the dead hand of the NASA bureaucracy is out of the way, will visionary billionaires inspired by [author and philosopher] Ayn Rand inaugurate a new age of commercial space travel for the masses?

Don't count on it. There might be a niche market for a few space-planes or rockets to take bored plutocrats into orbit for a joy ride. But investors would be wiser to invest in private bathyscaphes offering tours of the Marianas Trench. After 9/11 [September 11, 2001, terrorist attacks on the United States], can anyone believe that the world's governments are going to foster a regime of laissez-faire toward private space shuttles that could be hijacked for suicide missions from orbit, or that might disintegrate over several time zones?

And then there is the problem noted by the late William F. Buckley Jr. Because of security precautions, he joked, the increase of speed with each new mode of transport is neutralized by waiting times. A plane is faster than a train or bus, but you have to get to the airport two hours in advance. A spaceplane might take you across the continent in an hour—but you would have to arrive at the spaceport the day before.

In the next few generations there will probably be more human spaceflight on a small scale. In time there might even be tiny teams of scientists in orbit, on the moon or other planets, like those in Antarctica. But for the foreseeable future space exploration will be undertaken mainly by machines that don't horrify a watching world when they die slowly, with no hope of rescue.

The epitaph for the dream of human travel to outer space might be borrowed from [author] Samuel Johnson's verdict on a natural monument, the Giant's Causeway, in Ireland. It is worth seeing, he said, but it is not worth going to see.

VIEWPOINT 5

> *"It is important for us to pursue, and solve, the deepest questions of the universe, just as it is important for us to explore our solar system and eventually live beyond the confines of our home planet."*

Human Spaceflight Should Not End

Russell Prechtl and George Whitesides

Russell Prechtl is a US Air Force pilot, and George Whitesides is the national director of the National Space Society. In the following viewpoint, they maintain that human spaceflight is essential to the US space program for a number of reasons. First, human spaceflight will lead to the colonization of space and the survival of the human race in case of a catastrophe. Second, it spurs scientific discoveries and technological progress that help the human race. Finally, human spaceflight satisfies a need human beings have to explore the last frontier.

As you read, consider the following questions:

1. According to the authors, what has Steven Hawking expressed about space exploration?

Russell Prechtl and George Whitesides, "Commentary: The Value of Human Spaceflight," Space.com, September 28, 2007. www.space.com.

2. What do the authors list as examples of "spin-offs" from the space program?
3. What global movement do the authors assert came from early manned spaceflight?

Mr. Steven Weinberg has long been a vocal critic of NASA's manned spaceflight program, recently questioning the scientific usefulness of the International Space Station in particular, and asserting that the entire manned spaceflight program has produced nothing of scientific value.

The National Space Society, composed of members who promote mankind's future of living and working in space, strongly supports NASA's manned spaceflight program, and disagrees with both the spirit and substance of his comments.

The Need for Manned Spaceflight

For a first response, we turn to another renowned physicist, Dr. Stephen Hawking, who has urged the human race to "spread out into space for the survival of the species." Hawking states the increasing risk of being wiped out by a disaster, such as sudden global warming, nuclear war, or some other unknown danger as the primary reasons to diversify humanity's future beyond earth.

NASA has numerous examples of "spin-offs" from the space program, such as kidney dialysis machines, fetal heart monitors, programmable heart pacemakers, to name just a few that help Americans every day. Additionally the International Space Station operations enable NASA to learn valuable scientific information about the long-term effect of spaceflight on the human body, and how best to help humans adapt themselves for long trips, either in interplanetary space, or en route to planets such as Mars.

While these are all important, they don't compare to the effect these achievements have on the human spirit. Many of us still remember the first time we saw Earth from the Moon's

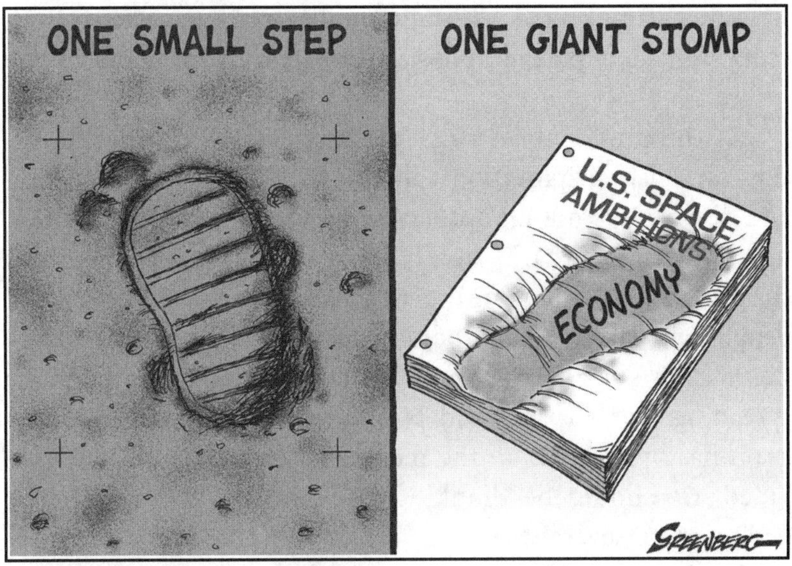

"Giant Stomp," cartoon by Steve Greenberg, www.CartoonStock.com.

orbit, when the astronauts of Apollo 8 filmed it on Christmas Eve, in 1968. Many argue this global awareness started the conservation movement, which might turn out to be the space program's greatest spin-off, and may save the earth's climate in the long run. Many of us were inspired when we saw the astronauts walk on the Moon, and realized that if mankind could do that, we could do almost anything. The achievements of NASA's unmanned spacecraft are phenomenal, and deserving of acclaim, but they don't lift people's spirits to these heights.

Investments in Our Future

Weinberg should understand that many citizens don't understand the benefits of theoretical physics to their own lives, and question the utility of the nation's investment in such work. That is an alternate explanation to why the Superconducting Super Collider was de-funded: Congress was not convinced of the utility of spending $12 billion on the project. Here is where we can observe a certain parallel with spaceflight: Both spaceflight and particle physics are basic investments in the future.

As the president [George W. Bush] stated during his Vision for Space Exploration speech, "The cause of exploration and discovery is not an option we choose; it is a desire written in the human heart." The National Space Society members support living and working in space, and the hundreds of people who have already bought their own suborbital spaceflight tickets are further proof that this is a vision that is spreading. For all the good NASA's manned spaceflight program has brought us, at the meager budget levels they're provided, we should be thanking and praising them for their dedicated perseverance.

It is not possible to predict all of the benefits that either the human space program or particle physics research will do for our country, but that does not mean that the searches are not worthy. It is important for us to pursue, and solve, the deepest questions of the universe, just as it is important for us to explore our solar system and eventually live beyond the confines of our home planet. Our descendents will thank us for both pursuits.

Viewpoint 6

"A human landing on Mars is the kind of mission—difficult but doable—that renews a society's sense of what it can accomplish."

NASA Should Shoot for a Human Landing on Mars

Loren Thompson

Loren Thompson is the chief operating officer at the Lexington Institute. In the following viewpoint, he derides the Barack Obama administration's plan to rearrange NASA's research and exploration priorities. Thompson claims that the new plan lacks a clear and urgent vision of the future of human spaceflight and cancels the Constellation program, which effectively ends the goal of a human landing on Mars. Thompson fears eliminating the possibility of human flights to Mars in the near future will mean the further decline of the US human spaceflight program.

As you read, consider the following questions:

1. What technology would the Constellation program have developed, according to Thompson?

2. What part of President Obama's plan does the author believe is the most politically controversial?
3. What is the latest thinking about how NASA should use its new technology, according to the author?

Of all the initiatives that President [Barack] Obama has begun during his first two years in office, none is more likely to be remembered a hundred years from today than the effort to rearrange NASA's research and exploration priorities. The reason why, unfortunately, is that it may signal the end of the road for one of the greatest technological achievements of modern times, the U.S. human spaceflight program. In place of a plan crafted by his predecessor which might have one day carried astronauts to Mars, Mr. Obama has proposed a science fair that literally goes nowhere.

The thousands of workers in NASA's human spaceflight program now in danger of losing their jobs should have seen this coming. Back when Obama was contending for the Democratic presidential nomination, his campaign floated a plan to divert billions of dollars from the astronaut program to education. Informed by his advisors that winning the support of space workers around Cape Canaveral was important to carrying Florida in the primaries, Obama beat a hasty retreat. But once in office, the new president did little to bring civil space expertise into the White House.

The Fate of Constellation

The key turning point came in February of this year [2010], when the administration proposed cancellation of a program inherited from the [George W.] Bush years called Constellation. Constellation would have developed a heavy-lift launch vehicle, crew capsule, and other technology needed to return astronauts to the Moon, and then eventually carry them on to Mars. The program wasn't highly imaginative, but it had one thing that every big technology initiative must have to be taken seriously: a goal. Taking astronauts to Mars would have revitalized NASA's faltering human spaceflight program after years of setbacks, because the Red Planet is the only destination in our solar system interesting enough to justify the cost of getting people there.

Of course, just getting people there wasn't the real point. Once the capability to go existed, the prospect of regular visits, and then a permanent colony, would beckon. Mars is more like Earth than any other place in the known universe, and while astronomers now believe there may be millions of Earth-like planets in our galaxy, Mars is the only one that is within reach. In fact, with all the technological advances in the four decades since Neil Armstrong first stepped onto the Moon, it's probably easier for astronauts to get to Mars (and back) today than it was to get to the Moon when President [John F.] Kennedy proposed a lunar landing in 1961.

Dismantling a Dream

But Barack Obama, as Senator Lloyd Bentsen might have put it, is no Jack Kennedy. He's a technocrat. The smartest technocrat in the room, maybe, but not a fellow who's real good at connecting technology initiatives to the aspirations of the American people. So Obama's alternative to Constellation was a collection of nice-to-have technologies with no clear purpose. No return trip to the Moon, no ultimate destination of Mars. Just a bunch of neat stuff. Obama defenders now say he had Mars in mind, but that goal wasn't spelled out when his plans were released. Instead, the new approach looked like the world's biggest science fair, at a time when the government was spending four billion dollars per day it did not have.

The Role of Russian Launch Vehicles

The most politically controversial part of the plan was the proposal to make American astronauts dependent on pricey Russian launch vehicles to get to the international space station, at least until U.S. entrepreneurs could come up with a low-cost alternative means of transit. Relying on the Russians was unavoidable given the impending retirement of the Space Shuttle, but it wasn't likely to bolster popular support for the human spaceflight program. And it turned out those U.S. "entrepreneurs" needed billions of dollars from the federal government to develop rockets based on old technology before they could take over from the Russians. Obviously, these fellows are not on the Edison plan.

But beyond those disagreeable details, what's really missing from the Obama plan is any sense of urgency or vision about where the whole human spaceflight enterprise is headed. For instance, the plan calls for spending several years researching a new heavy-lift launch vehicle for deep space exploration before committing to a design—a stretched-out schedule that would likely produce little new technology but deprive engineering teams and production workers of anything to do for the better part of a decade. Since I'm not a conspiracy theorist I won't suggest that this element of the plan seems well-crafted to eliminate any political constituency for future deep space missions, but it sure takes a long time to make key decisions.

Finding Alternatives

Congress was not happy with the plan, and has struggled to come up with a way of keeping unique technical expertise intact. It will probably direct that development of a new heavy-lift launch vehicle begin much sooner based on technology already in hand, and that the crew capsule being developed for the cancelled Constellation program be retained for other purposes. But Congress doesn't have a great track record on formulating alternatives to presidential space initiatives, mainly because its efforts get dissipated in trying to keep many local constituencies happy.

The latest, relatively lame, thinking is that NASA should use whatever new technology is funded to attempt a manned landing on an asteroid. I can't say what the scientific value of such a mission would be, but I can say this: proposing a human landing on Mars in 2030 would be a lot more inspiring. Not only is Mars potentially capable of supporting life, but its Earth-like qualities would enable any mission there to generate more important scientific findings. It's a lot harder to get there and back, but the scientific rewards are correspondingly greater.

A human landing on Mars is the kind of mission—difficult but doable—that renews a society's sense of what it can accomplish. And Mars really is the only destination that can prevent the kind of funding the manned spaceflight program will require from becoming fatally controversial in the current fiscal environment. The simple reality is that if the Obama administration and Congress don't make Mars the goal, NASA's human spaceflight program isn't likely to last much longer.

VIEWPOINT 7

"All that is needed is a little innovation, and to break out of the mind-set of the Apollo Cargo Cult, in which anything that doesn't resemble Apollo—a specific destination, a date, and a really big rocket—isn't a real human exploration program."

NASA Has More Important Priorities than a Human Landing on Mars

Iain Murray and Rand Simberg

Iain Murray is an author and heads the Center for Economic Freedom at the Competitive Enterprise Institute. Rand Simberg is an aerospace engineer and a consultant in space commercialization, space tourism, and Internet security. In the following viewpoint, they suggest that criticism over the cancellation of the Constellation program and the Barack Obama administration's reordering of NASA priorities is misplaced. Murray and Simberg argue that critics of the new NASA priorities must realize that the United States must effectively harness private enterprise to remain at the forefront of space exploration and development in

Iain Murray and Rand Simberg, "Big Government's Final Frontier," *American Spectator*, November 10, 2010. Copyright © The American Spectator 2010. Reproduced by permission.

the future. Implementing these new priorities will open up new partnerships and opportunities for NASA and space entrepreneurs.

As you read, consider the following questions:

1. How do the authors describe the Constellation program?
2. According to the authors, how long will the United States be involved with the International Space Station under the new plan?
3. What misconception do the authors believe has been a major stumbling block for space missions ever since humans last walked on the moon?

There's something about space policy that makes conservatives forget their principles. Just one mention of NASA, and conservatives are quite happy to check their small-government instincts at the door and vote in favor of massive government programs and harsh regulations that stifle private enterprise. It's time to abort that mission.

A Misunderstanding of the Constellation Program

Loren Thompson, writing in the *Forbes Business in the Beltway* blog, recently suggested that President [Barack] Obama's space policy represents the "end of the road" for U.S. manned spaceflight. Yet Thompson is simply repeating a defense of pork barrel politics that would play well in Huntsville or Houston. Moreover, his claim that President [George W.] Bush had a plan that "might have one day carried astronauts to Mars," while Obama's version is "a science fair that literally goes nowhere," misrepresents both plans.

The cancelled Constellation program, former NASA administrator Mike Griffin's flawed implementation of Bush's Vision for Space Exploration, focused on the moon, and was an unaffordable redo of Apollo, with no capability or plans to go to Mars, and poor prospects for returning to the moon for that matter. What Mr. Thompson derides as a "science fair" is the development of new technologies that will enable affordable visits not just to the moon, but to asteroids, the moons of Mars, the Martian surface, and points beyond—at much lower cost.

On its cost and schedule trajectory, Constellation would have created a gap of at least seven years—until 2017 at the earliest—during which we would have had to continue to purchase Soyuz launches and capsules from Russia, to use for crew change-outs and as lifeboats for the International Space Station [ISS]. This is particularly ironic, because under the Bush plans, the ISS itself would be abandoned two years earlier, in 2015!

New Opportunities

On the other hand, with the new plans, U.S. involvement with the ISS will continue until at least 2020 (and probably beyond). New commercial capabilities to deliver astronauts both to the station and to low-Earth orbit for exploration beyond would become available no later than 2015 (and probably earlier), at a small fraction of the cost of the planned Constellation rocket: the Ares I launcher and Orion crew capsule.

The new NASA plan would make those capabilities available not just to a few NASA civil servants, but to all comers, including private space researchers and sovereign clients (foreign governments) that have signed memoranda of understanding with Bigelow Aerospace to lease its planned orbital facilities, independent of the ISS.

The U.S. will thereby become a seller of human space transportation services, instead of a supplicant to and pur-

A Brief History of Mars Exploration

Many robots from Earth have probed Mars. The United States, Russia, Europe and Japan over four decades have sent numerous flybys, orbiters and landers to Mars.

On December 2, 1971, the Soviet Union's Mars 3 was the first spacecraft to make a successful soft landing on Mars.

Later, three American spacecraft completed highly successful landings on the surface—the pair of Viking landers in 1976 and Mars Pathfinder 21 years later in 1997.

In addition, several spacecraft have either flown by the Red Planet, sending back picture postcards as they traveled on, or have dropped successfully into orbit around Mars.

Numerous other Mars spacecraft over the years either failed to leave Earth at all or were unable to find their way correctly to the Red Planet.

In the 21st century, five probes from America, Europe and Japan have flown to Mars, including Europe's and Japan's first solo missions to Mars.

"Exploring Mars,"
Space Today Online, *2006.*
www.spacetoday.org.

chaser of them from Russia. Call us crazy, but the former plan looks a lot more like the "end of U.S. human spaceflight" than does the latter.

The Benefits of Private Enterprise

When Thompson writes that "those U.S. 'entrepreneurs' needed billions of dollars from the federal government to develop rockets based on old technology before they could take over from the Russians," we can only shake our heads sadly.

First, there is no reason for the scare quotes around "entrepreneurs." Space Exploration Technologies [SpaceX] has invested hundreds of millions of its own money to develop its Falcon launcher and Dragon capsule, scheduled to fly next month [December 2010], for a tiny fraction of the projected cost of Ares/Orion. SpaceX has a huge backlog of orders. In fact, to meet its ISS obligations as soon and cost effectively as possible, NASA needs SpaceX and other commercial crew providers more than SpaceX needs NASA.

Thompson also suggests that NASA's scrapped plans did not involve "old technology," when in fact the program was premised on reusing Shuttle components—and thus maintaining their associated jobs, which is why the Shuttle program [Space Transportation System] has remained so expensive and was so popular with politicians.

Another Misconception

Finally, when Thompson complains about the long development time for the planned heavy lifter, he implies that such a vehicle is necessary for human exploration beyond Earth orbit. That misconception has been a major stumbling block for such missions ever since humans last walked on the moon almost 40 years ago.

In fact, the United Launch Alliance, a joint venture of Boeing and Lockheed Martin, has developed and described viable mission scenarios in which lunar missions can be accomplished with existing launch systems. All that is needed is a little innovation, and to break out of the mind-set of the Apollo Cargo Cult, in which anything that doesn't resemble Apollo—a specific destination, a date, and a really big rocket—isn't a real human exploration program.

It is time for conservatives to recognize that Apollo is over. We must recognize that Apollo was a centrally planned monopolistic government program for a few government employees, in the service of Cold War propaganda and was therefore itself an affront to American values. If we want to seriously explore, and potentially exploit space, we need to harness private enterprise, and push the technologies really needed to do so.

VIEWPOINT 8

> *"Establishing a proper base on the moon would be a huge and challenging undertaking."*

NASA Should Establish a Moon Base

Hal G.P. Colebatch

Hal G.P. Colebatch is an author and a commentator. In the following viewpoint, he contends that if the United States is interested in exploring and eventually working and living on other planets, the logical first step to that goal would be to establish a base on the moon. Colebatch points out that such a base would advance scientific research substantially. He also notes that with other countries expressing interest in establishing a moon base, it would be within US national security interests to pursue one as well.

As you read, consider the following questions:

1. What does the author say the letter written by former astronauts Neil Armstrong, James Lovell, and Eugene Cernan contends about the new NASA priorities?
2. According to the author, when did the British government kill off their space program?

3. Why does the author believe that the moon is a ready-made space station?

Any long-term future for the U.S. in space has suddenly become a great deal less assured, despite the fact spaceflight has been paying massive dividends for decades. President [Barack] Obama, to the joy of some rivals and enemies of the U.S. Space program, has produced a future of fudge for it, which upon examination looks as if it is no future at all. Apparently, according to the president, the U.S. is not going back to the moon because it's already been there, but it's going somewhere else. Where exactly is a moot point:

Obama has been reported as saying:

> Now, I understand that some believe that we should attempt a return to the surface of the Moon first, as previously planned, but I just have to say pretty bluntly here: We've been there before. Fifty years after the creation of NASA, our goal is no longer just a destination to reach. Our goal is the capacity for people to work and learn and operate and live safely beyond the Earth for extended periods of time, ultimately in ways that are more sustainable and even indefinite.

Like so many of Obama's speeches, it sounds good at first, with something in it for everyone. Except that at a second look, there doesn't seem to be anything in it for anyone, least of all the space program. It sounds less like a program for exploring space than for putting off space exploration as jam tomorrow and, literally, pie in the sky. It also seems to fit uncomfortably well with, to use old-fashioned language, a turning away from the concept to manifest destiny, which surfaces in Obama's thoughts and actions at times.

Opposition to the Obama Plan

Neil Armstrong and fellow Apollo 11 program commanders James Lovell and Eugene Cernan have released a letter saying that while some of Mr. Obama's NASA budget proposals have merit, the decision to cancel the Constellation program, the Ares I and Ares V rockets and the Orion spacecraft is devastating.

American astronauts could now only reach low Earth orbit and the International Space Station by hitching a ride on the Russian Soyuz spacecraft at a price of more than $50 million per seat, the letter said.

It continued:

> For the United States, the leading spacefaring nation for nearly half a century, to be without carriage to low Earth orbit and with no human exploration capability to go beyond Earth orbit for an indeterminate time into the future, destines our nation to become one of second- or even third-rate stature. . . .
>
> Without the skill and experience that actual spacecraft operation provides, the USA is far too likely to be on a long downhill slide to mediocrity.

Britain provides a historic example. Socialist Prime Minister Harold Wilson (who once promised: "We are restating our socialism in terms of the scientific revolution . . . the Britain that is going to be forged in the white heat of this revolution will be no place for . . . outdated methods.") and left-wing Conservative Prime Minister Edward Heath between them killed off a successful and inexpensive British space program in the 1970s with its own rockets and satellites (and which, if proceeded with, would have been a financial Golconda). There was never the money or, more importantly, the will and inspiration, to start it again. It drifted off into the realms of "one day . . .", becoming ever more remote. A tiny British space agency has only just been restarted and its future seems vague and uncertain (this in a country which each year spends enough on gambling to finance the U.S. Space program).

Establishing a proper base on the moon would be a huge and challenging undertaking. Establishing a base somewhere else—Mars or the asteroids—would be many times more difficult, expensive, and dangerous. This is not to say it couldn't, or shouldn't, be done eventually—it certainly should and inevitably someone is going to do it eventually—but to bypass the moon, a case of running before one can walk, is simply bizarre. If the U.S.'s goal really is "for people to work and learn and operate and live safely beyond the Earth for extended periods of time," the moon is the obvious place to learn how to do it.

Obama's reported reason for abandoning the moon project—"We've been there before"—if taken seriously, and U.S. presidential policy pronouncements are meant to be taken seriously—is simply horrifying in its myopia, ignorance and philistinism. It is as if 16th-century Spain refused any further funding for exploring the Americas on the grounds that Columbus had already reached it ("But one day we'll go to the North Pole").

Twelve men have landed on the moon and stayed for a few hours, the last more than 40 years ago. They brought back some rock samples. This was important but in terms of advancing science did not even scratch the surface of what could be done.

The Chinese, it seems, appreciate the potential scientific and possibly military value of the moon. They have launched four manned rockets, the last carrying two men, and it is reasonable to guess that they are aiming at a permanent moonbase. India, Europe, and of course Russia are all pushing into space, while the U.S. throws away its lead.

In fact, the moon is a ready-made space station. Its low gravity means large spacecraft can be assembled there relatively easily for longer voyages. As a major bonus large quantities of water have recently been found there—a heavy and incompressible substance difficult to transport into space: you can't save weight or space in a spaceship's stores by carrying compressed or dehydrated water. The mere fact of working in

Why Should the United States Return to the Moon?

1. Human Civilization

Extend human presence to the moon to enable eventual settlement.

2. Scientific Knowledge

Pursue scientific activities that address fundamental questions about the history of Earth, the solar system and the universe—and about our place in them.

3. Exploration Preparation

Test technologies, systems, flight operations and exploration techniques to reduce the risks and increase the productivity of future missions to Mars and beyond.

4. Global Partnerships

Provide a challenging, shared and peaceful activity that unites nations in pursuit of common objectives.

5. Economic Expansion

Expand Earth's economic sphere, and conduct lunar activities with benefits to life on the home planet.

6. Public Engagement

Use a vibrant space exploration program to engage the public, encourage students and help develop the high-tech workforce that will be required to address the challenges of tomorrow.

NASA, "Why the Moon?," May 22, 2011. www.nasa.gov.

vacuum might well establish a whole set of new industries and technologies. It is simply impossible to know what benefits and innovations a moon-base would bring, but it is safe to say that, like the space program itself, they would be substantial.

The Problem with Mars

Further, while an operating moon-base might be a practical demonstration of the value of spaceflight, as artificial satellites have been, with all sorts of unforeseen benefits, it is hard to imagine the money ever being available for a one-off shot straight to Mars. What it looks like is administering euthanasia to the space program while disguising the fact in pseudo-stirring language of exploration, adventure, and discovery. It is also hard to imagine "astronaut" being first choice for a career-option among the best and brightest when the possibility of getting into space, let alone of setting foot on another world, is suddenly decades away, if it still exists at all.

Jerry de Groot, a British professor of history with an extreme dislike of spaceflight, has, in a series of anti-space diatribes, likened spaceflight to "carrion" and a sign of America's "spiritual vacuity." One thing he has written, however, is all too plausible. He claims:

> Obama has promised a radical overhaul of space policy. And pigs might fly . . .
>
> The president, however, hasn't the guts to pull the plug on the manned program. Therefore, he has decided to fudge. NASA will be given an additional $6 billion over the next five years to develop the technologies to take human beings to the Moon and beyond. Since a mission to Mars is conservatively costed at $500 billion, the money will pay for a few blueprints.
>
> Obama's new version of the fudge can be easily explained. While most Americans have grown contemptuous of funding space spectaculars [Oh, really?], the voters of Florida remain enthusiastic, for obvious reasons. Those who work in the space industry might talk passionately of man's need to explore, but what they really want is a wage packet. And, as recent elections have clearly demonstrated, no president can

afford to annoy the Floridians. I suspect the fudge will continue long after Obama retires. Landing on Mars will always be an event scheduled to occur 20 years from tomorrow.

Periodical and Internet Sources Bibliography

The following articles have been selected to supplement the diverse views presented in this chapter.

Waleed Abdalati and Robert Braun	"After Space Shuttle Program, NASA's Future Still Bright," *Baltimore Sun*, July 4, 2011.
Bob Burnett	"Lost in Space: The Decline of the American Spirit," *Huffington Post*, July 15, 2011.
Jesse Clark	"The Future of Space Exploration," *San Diego Union-Tribune Chronicle*, July 28, 2011.
Walter Cunningham	"Taking a Bite Out of NASA," *Houston Chronicle*, February 6, 2010.
Julie Johnsson	"NASA's Future Cloudy as U.S. Plans to Shift Focus in Space Exploration," *Chicago Tribune*, March 21, 2010.
Irene Klotz	"Shuttles' End Stirs Doubts About U.S. Space Program," Reuters, July 5, 2011. www.reuters.com.
Ray Kwong	"U.S. Boldly Goes No More as China's Space Program Takes Off," *Forbes*, July 7, 2011. www.forbes.com.
John M. Logsdon	"The U.S. Space Program's Leadership Black Hole," *Washington Post*, July 11, 2011.
Owen Matthews and Anna Nemtsova	"Russians Win the Space Race," *Daily Beast*, July 8, 2011.
Bob Orr	"Astronaut John Glenn Mulls Space Program Future," CBS News, July 5, 2011. www.cbsnews.com.
Seth Shostak	"American Space Research: An Also-Ran?," *Huffington Post*, July 17, 2011.

OPPOSING VIEWPOINTS® SERIES

Chapter 2

What Issues Surround the Space Shuttle Program?

Chapter Preface

On July 21, 2011, the space shuttle *Atlantis* landed at its home port, NASA's Kennedy Space Center in Florida. It had spent twelve days in space, during which it successfully delivered vital supplies to the International Space Station. For many scientists, astronauts, policy makers, and space enthusiasts, the end of the *Atlantis* mission was bittersweet—it signaled the end of the US space shuttle program. NASA had decided to shutter the program and pursue a new direction in space exploration.

NASA's space shuttle program, officially called the Space Transportation System (STS), was conceived as a less expensive, more convenient way to transport people and supplies to space stations. Planning of the STS started as early as the late 1960s, before the Apollo 11 moon landing. The program was officially launched on January 5, 1972, when President Richard Nixon announced that NASA was developing a reusable space shuttle.

"I have decided today that the United States should proceed at once with the development of an entirely new type of space transportation system designed to help transform the space frontier of the 1970s into familiar territory, easily accessible for human endeavor in the 1980s and '90s," Nixon stated in his 1972 speech. "This system will center on a space vehicle that can shuttle repeatedly from Earth to orbit and back. It will revolutionize transportation into near space, by routinizing it. It will take the astronomical costs out of astronautics. In short, it will go a long way toward delivering the rich benefits of practical space utilization and the valuable spin-offs from space efforts into the daily lives of Americans and all people."

By 1976, NASA had built an orbiter, which was named the *Enterprise*. Although it never flew in orbit, it proved invaluable in testing the design of the shuttle. In 1979, the first fully functioning orbiter, the *Columbia*, was completed. It was launched to fanfare on April 12, 1981, marking an exciting day in NASA history. Within years, other orbiters would follow the *Columbia* into space: the *Challenger* (first launched April 4, 1983), the *Discovery* (August 30, 1984), the *Atlantis* (October 3, 1985), and the *Endeavour* (May 7, 1992).

The shuttle is a remarkable technological achievement. It is the only winged, manned spacecraft to achieve orbit and land. It is reusable and was used for multiple flights into orbit. It performed vital tasks, like conducting manned scientific experiments in orbit; servicing the Hubble Space Telescope, including replacing aging and malfunctioning equipment; building and transporting crews and supplies to the International Space Station; and carrying satellites into space.

With its impressive record of accomplishment, there have also been a few heartbreaking tragedies that have affected the space shuttle program. On January 28, 1986, the *Challenger* broke up shortly after takeoff, killing all seven crew members. It was later found that the accident was due to a faulty O-ring, a part used to seal off the solid-fuel rocket booster. The loss of the *Challenger* shocked the world. Many people were watching the shuttle launch on live television and were distraught at the thought of the brave astronauts losing their lives. President Ronald Reagan gave a speech later that day, remarking, "I know it is hard to understand, but sometimes painful things like this happen. It's all part of the process of exploration and discovery. It's all part of taking a chance and expanding man's horizons. The future doesn't belong to the fainthearted; it belongs to the brave. The *Challenger* crew was pulling us into the future, and we'll continue to follow them."

Tragedy struck the program again on February 1, 2003, when the *Columbia* broke apart over Texas on its reentry into Earth's atmosphere, killing all seven astronauts aboard. Investigations of the accident showed that a piece of foam installation had broken off during the launch and damaged the shuttle's thermal protection system. When the *Columbia* reentered the atmosphere, the shuttle could not protect itself from the tremendous heat and disintegrated.

Following the *Columbia* tragedy, space shuttle missions were suspended for two years. In 2004, President George W. Bush announced his Vision for Space Exploration, which envisioned retiring the space shuttle program after the completion of the International Space Station in 2010. The successor to the space shuttle would be Project Constellation, which included two launch vehicles and the Orion spacecraft. The Constellation would take over the shuttle duties and have more capabilities than the shuttle. In 2010, however, President Barack Obama proposed a revised plan for the Constellation that included more private sector involvement.

As the space shuttle program came to a close in 2011, NASA administrator Charles Bolden offered a glowing assessment. "The space shuttle is an amazing vehicle, and the incredible program it pioneered has taught us many things and helped make tomorrow's exploration possible," he remarked.

The following chapter examines recent controversies surrounding NASA's space shuttle program. Viewpoints debate the end of the program, the role of the private sector in space transportation, the performance of the shuttle, and the locations for the retired space shuttles.

Viewpoint 1

"The space shuttle itself is an amazing feat of engineering, has brought about many scientific advances, and has deepened our knowledge about the galaxy. But it has largely failed to spark the national imagination."

It Is the Right Time to End the Space Shuttle Program

Hanna Rosin

Hanna Rosin is a contributing editor for the Atlantic. *In the following viewpoint, she discerns a widespread apathy to the space shuttle program that has cemented its recent cancellation. With the Cold War over, America has lost its passion for the shuttle program. Rosin notes that people are more excited about technological advances that maximize our efficiency than exploration of the great unknown, and that is where the money and resources will go.*

As you read, consider the following questions:

1. What did Rosin say newspaper reports of the *Atlantis* mission make NASA sound like?

Hanna Rosin, "Earthbound," *Atlantic Monthly*, September 2010.

2. What did Barack Obama say about plans to retire the shuttle program?
3. What did Lyndon Johnson say about the Cold War space race?

The launch of a space shuttle can still make you weep with amazement and wonder, if you happen to be watching it. In May [2010], my family and I stood with a group of thousands at Cape Canaveral waiting for one of the last planned launches (the last is tentatively scheduled for early next year [2011]). It was hot and we were penned in to a set of bleachers a few miles away, and yet no one seemed to be complaining about heat or thirst. We sang the national anthem and counted down in tandem with the giant red numbers on a clock. It seemed impossible that such a large, heavy object could leave the ground or that any people would agree to go with it, given past disasters, and yet they did. The ground rumbled and the orbiter *Atlantis* shot off in a straight line, going up and up until it disappeared out of sight, leaving a trail of white smoke. We looked up into the sky for what seemed like hours (it was about three minutes), until it was gone. "Where'd it go?" one kid asked her father. "Poof," he answered, and even to us adults, that made sense—it felt as if Dumbledore [a major protagonist in the Harry Potter series], or maybe God, had grabbed that rocket and the six men inside and taken them to another dimension, leaving only smoke and awe behind.

The Thrill Is Gone

Merely reading about a shuttle launch cannot remotely convey that same kind of thrill. The wire stories about the *Atlantis*'s liftoff, which were picked up mostly by smaller newspapers, explained that its mission was to deliver cargo and spare parts to the International Space Station, including six new batteries to provide station power; the details made NASA sound like a

"Unemployed Space Shuttle," cartoon by Mike Flinn, www.CartoonStock.com.

sort of giant intergalactic hardware store offering delivery service. When the shuttle returned 12 days later, news stories mentioned that it might find a proper home in a museum. In April, President Barack Obama traveled to Kennedy Space Center to confirm that he will stick with plans to retire the shuttle program. "We can't just keep on doing the same old things that we've been doing," he said. He also defended his plan to cancel Constellation, NASA's next program for manned spaceflight, which he has called "lacking in innovation." (Congress has not yet agreed, and Obama did confirm his commitment to deep-space exploration and a future mission to Mars, but we're a long way away from launching such a trip.) The space shuttle itself is an amazing feat of engineering, has brought about many scientific advances, and has deepened our knowledge about the galaxy. But it has largely failed to spark the national imagination. From the perspective of space enthusiasts, the whole program seems to have done "the same relatively minor experiments over and over," says Louis Friedman, executive director of the Planetary Society. What human space exploration needs, Friedman rightly points out, is a "better story."

Back in the 1960s, the story was obvious. Space travel tapped into the grand narrative of our dominance over the Russians in the larger battle between good and evil. In the movie version of *The Right Stuff*, one of the test pilots describes the sound barrier as a "demon" who lives in the sky and had to be conquered, while the Lyndon B. Johnson character says, "I, for one, don't want to go to sleep by the light of a Communist moon." But the Cold War is long over, and to some extent, so too is the idea of limitless national possibility. These days, the technological advances that get us fired up have to do not with outward exploration but with maximizing our own efficiency—better and more-versatile phones, for instance.

The Glory Days

When my family and I were touring the NASA facilities, we caught glimpses of the old glory days. NASA projects often have romantic names that link into a long history of exploration and adventure: *Atlantis* and *Discovery*, for example. The astronauts roaming the grounds still carry the aura of heroes, particularly for the children, who gasped every time they saw one. Awesome pictures from the Hubble [Space] Telescope line the halls, offering a window into our galaxy and beyond. NASA books and merchandise in the gift shop raise profound philosophical questions: "Imagine knowing that we are not alone, but that life is abundant in our solar system and throughout the universe."

But the most compelling story unfolding was a human one that brought us very much back to Earth. In one facility, I talked to an engineer who was checking the tiles on a shuttle being prepared for the next launch. What would he be doing once the program ends, I asked him. "Standing on the unemployment lines," he said.

VIEWPOINT 2

> *"Four or five more years of shuttle flights—say, ten additional missions all told—would not seem unreasonable."*

Private Companies Could Keep Space Shuttles Flying

N.V.

N.V. is a correspondent for the Babbage *blog on the* Economist *website. In the following viewpoint, the correspondent discusses a proposal from United Space Alliance, a venture between Boeing and Lockheed Martin, to continue flying the two youngest space shuttles, the* Atlantis *and* Endeavour. *There would be two advantages to such a plan: Americans would not have to rely on Russian vehicles to transport American astronauts and technology, and it would avoid the controversy as to where the retired space shuttles will be assigned. N.V. contends that if Congress finds the money to build new external fuel tanks for the shuttles, the proposed plan is viable and advantageous to the US space program.*

As you read, consider the following questions:

1. What does the author view as the city most associated with the American space program?

N.V., "The Difference Engine: Houston, We Have a Problem," *Economist*, April 21, 2011.

2. According to the author, why should the National Museum of the US Air Force at Wright-Patterson Air Force Base get a retired shuttle?
3. How many flights did the *Discovery* clock before it was retired?

Which city, in the whole of the United States, would the average person associate most clearly with America's towering achievements, and no few sorrows, over the past half century of sending men and women into space? Why, Houston, of course—home of the Johnson Space Center, where NASA's mission control is located. We know this from all that has been said and done in the past. The first words Neil Armstrong uttered as Apollo 11 touched down on the Moon in 1969 were: "Houston, Tranquility base here—the *Eagle* has landed."

Houston Gets Left Out

The name of Houston will forever be associated with the manned exploration of space. No astronaut ever radioed laconically back from a crippled spaceship, "Manhattan, we have a problem". Yet, in NASA's recent selection of the final destinations for its four extant space shuttles, now that the last operational ones are about to be pensioned off, New York City will get *Enterprise*, the first of the shuttles that was rolled out in 1976, while Houston gets snubbed.

A score or more of museums and other institutions around the country competed for the honour of having a shuttle in their permanent collection. Apart from offering an appealing display, each had to be ready to stump up $28.8m [million] to cover the cost of preparing and transporting the winged spacecraft to its new location. Of the three other remaining shuttles, *Discovery* is destined for the Smithsonian's National Air and Space Museum annex outside Washington, DC. After the launch in late June of the 135th (and last) mission in the shuttle programme, *Atlantis* will remain in Florida to be exhibited at the Kennedy Space Center's visitor centre.

Meanwhile, after its own final mission later this month, *Endeavour*, the youngest of the shuttles, will be ferried to Los Angeles to end its days in the California Science Center, alongside existing exhibits of the Mercury, Gemini and Apollo spacecraft, and close to the old Rockwell plant in Palmdale where the shuttle was developed. Meanwhile, just up the road, at Edwards Air Force Base, is the runway where nearly half of all shuttle flights touched down.

A Baffling Decision

So, three shuttle exhibits on the East Coast, one on the West Coast, and nothing in between. The good citizens of Houston are rightly indignant about being deprived of their space-age heritage. And it is not just Texans who are irked by NASA's seemingly bizarre decision. Jason Chaffetz, a congressman from Utah (not Texas) has introduced a bill in the House of Representatives that would "restore common sense and fairness" and send one of the shuttles to Houston rather than New York. "Instead of relying on political guidance systems, these decisions must be steered by history and logic," Mr Chaffetz insists.

Others on Capitol Hill believe the National Museum of the US Air Force at Wright-Patterson Air Force Base, near Dayton, Ohio, also has a better claim than New York for a shuttle exhibit. The air force played a seminal role in bringing the shuttle into being. Indeed, much of the spacecraft's basic design—in particular, the size and shape of the cargo hold and the vehicle's ability to make 2,000km "detours" across range—was dictated by military requirements. "Locating a shuttle in Dayton would provide 60% of America's population with access within a day's drive," says Senator Sherrod Brown of Ohio. Senator Brown, a member of the influential Senate

Appropriations Committee, has called for a federal investigation into NASA's "flawed selection process".

Your correspondent is interested to learn the final resting places readers would personally choose for the four remaining shuttles. Presumably, most would agree to locate one at the Smithsonian, because of the museum's pre-eminence in preserving artifacts of American life, culture and achievement. But after that, should the choice be driven by history and heritage, or by proximity to large urban populations and convenience for visitors? If the former, then clearly both Cape Canaveral and Houston have legitimate claims. If the latter, then New York, Los Angeles and even Chicago should be considered. What should obviously not be allowed to influence the decision, though it invariably does, is the political clout of one region over another.

Houston: Home of Mission Control

For the record, it should be noted that Houston only became the home of mission control as a result of political wrangling at the highest level in the early 1960s. The original mission-control centre was at the Cape. But a bigger site was sought to accommodate the testing and research facilities needed for the Apollo mission to the moon. The Houston proposal met only half the criteria set for the new location, while several other sites had better qualifications all round, especially the Boston area of Massachusetts. However, backstage bullying by Lyndon Johnson—as the Senate majority leader from Texas and later as vice president and subsequently president—won the day for Houston. The Manned Spacecraft Center, which opened there in 1963, was renamed the Johnson Space Center in 1973 in honour of its political patron.

Enterprise

It should also be noted that *Enterprise*, the shuttle destined for New York, never actually flew in space. It was the first of six vehicles to be built, though not equipped for orbital flight—having no engines nor a working heat shield. It was carried aloft by a converted Boeing 747 and used solely for glide-approach and landing tests. Many of its components were later removed as spares for other shuttles.

Equipped with dummy replacement bits, *Enterprise* has been part of the Smithsonian's National Air and Space Museum collection since 1985, and on display at the museum's [Steven F.] Udvar-Hazy Center next door to Dulles International Airport, Virginia, since 2004. It will be shipped to New York City, to be exhibited alongside the *Intrepid* aircraft carrier moored off Pier 86. In its place, the Smithsonian will get the biggest prize of all: the venerable *Discovery*, the oldest and most travelled of the remaining orbiters (*Challenger* exploded minutes after launch in 1986, and *Columbia* disintegrated during re-entry in 2003, killing all seven crew members in each instance).

Would Houstonians be happy with such a cardboard cutout of a spacecraft as *Enterprise* has become? Your correspondent thinks not. Some say it is fit only for, if not New Yorkers, the Hollywood film sets of Los Angeles. By rights, they say, the spritely and technically advanced *Endeavour*—built to replace the lost *Challenger* largely from spare parts intended for other shuttles—should go to Houston, not Los Angeles.

A Plan to Keep the Shuttles Flying

There is a long shot that such an outcome just might happen. United Space Alliance, a Houston-based venture between Boeing and Lockheed Martin set up in 1995 to operate NASA's shuttle fleet, has put forward a plan to continue flying the two youngest orbiters, *Atlantis* and *Endeavour*, twice a year on a commercial basis. When the shuttle programme comes to a close this summer [in 2011], American astronauts will have to hitch a ride on Russian spacecraft to visit the International Space Station. In due course, NASA hopes to use commercial space vehicles developed by private companies such as Blue Origin, Sierra Nevada [Corporation], SpaceX and Boeing to carry American astronauts into orbit. But that is unlikely to happen until 2015 at the very earliest.

Four or five more years of shuttle flights—say, ten additional missions all told—would not seem ureasonable. *Atlantis* would then have completed 38 flights and *Endeavour* 30 (by the time it retired last month, *Discovery* had clocked up 39 flights). The only problem is that such a plan would require the construction of an entirely new external fuel tank. The plant for making the huge container that feeds the shuttle's engines during its ascent into orbit has closed and the tooling dismantled.

If, by some strange turn of events, Congress were to find the money to build a new external tank, the two shuttles still in use could see their operational lives extended. Then, the decision where ultimately to locate them, when their days were finally over, could be considered anew in the light of a wider informed opinion—yours included. After all, it was a write-in campaign by "Trekkies" that forced NASA to change the name of the first shuttle from *Constitution* to *Enterprise*. Your voice could yet be heard.

VIEWPOINT 3

"By 1980 the shuttle program had practically doubled its original budget; today, after three decades and almost $200 billion spent, it has missed almost every budget and performance goal."

The Space Shuttle Program Never Performed to Expectation

Pete Peterson

Pete Peterson is executive director of the Davenport Institute for Public Engagement and Civic Leadership at Pepperdine University's School of Public Policy. In the following viewpoint, he maintains that the space shuttle program should be considered a cautionary tale for all ambitious infrastructure projects. Peterson views the program as a series of fudged budget and performance numbers from the very beginning—these unrealistic numbers were used to get the project approved in the first place. He finds that such skewed projections and budget numbers are common to mega projects, such as the Big Dig in Boston or the Chunnel in western Europe.

Pete Peterson, "Of Space Ships and Bullet Trains," *City Journal*, April 6, 2011.

As you read, consider the following questions:

1. According to the author, what were the conclusions of the Columbia Accident Investigation Board?
2. What did Gregg Easterbrook's investigation into the space shuttle program show?
3. How much did Boston's Big Dig project run over budget, according to the author?

With the final landing of the space shuttle *Discovery* on March 9 [2011], a significant chapter in NASA history came to a close. It's the beginning of the end for the space shuttle program—the final flights of *Endeavour* and *Atlantis* are scheduled for later this year—and thus a fitting occasion to reflect on an effort that dates back to the [Richard] Nixon administration. As President [Barack] Obama calls for a new era of "doing big things"—from creating a high-speed rail system to building wind farms—the record of the shuttle program and other "mega projects" worldwide suggests a simple warning: beware the "unbiased expert."

Assessing the Space Shuttle Program

Commenting from Kennedy Space Center before *Discovery*'s final launch, *PBS Newshour*'s Miles O'Brien gave an unsentimental valediction for the shuttle program: "Well, the promise of the space shuttle program, when you look at how they were selling it in front of Congress, was just pure fancy. There were all these studies which indicated the space shuttle fleet could be flown on the order of once a week, and that it would have airliner-like capability for turning it around once it got on the ground. But it's an incredibly complicated system. And there wasn't a full appreciation at the time for really how difficult it was to fly a reusable spacecraft to and from space." O'Brien's skepticism has become more common since the October 2003 release of NASA's final report on the *Columbia* disaster. Investigating the causes of *Columbia*'s tragic disintegration over Texas on February 3, 2003, the Columbia Accident Investigation Board looked beyond the event itself, concluding that the accident's origins could be found three decades earlier, in the program's first days: "It is the Board's view that, in retrospect, the increased complexity of a shuttle designed to be all things to all people created inherently greater risks than if more realistic technical goals had been set at the start. . . . Throughout the history of the program, a gap has persisted between the rhetoric NASA has used to market the Space Shuttle and operational reality."

Fudged Numbers and Predictions

During the *Columbia* investigation, Robert F. Thompson, the shuttle program's manager from 1970 until just after its first launch in 1981, officially confirmed what many had long suspected: that from their first discussions with Nixon aides, NASA engineers and other interested parties had fudged budget and performance numbers. To gain congressional support for the multibillion-dollar project, NASA had to demonstrate that the shuttle would have a much lower cost "per payload pound" than conventional single-use rockets. As Thompson recounted in his testimony before the Columbia Accident Investigation Board on April 23, 2003: "At the time that we were *selling the program* [emphasis added] at the start of Phase B, the people in Washington got a company called Mathematica to come in and do an analysis of operating costs. Mathematica discovered that the more you flew, the cheaper it got per flight. Fabulous. . . . So they added as many flights as they could. They got up to 40 or 50 flights a year. Hell, anyone reasonable knew you weren't going to fly 50 times a year."

Not everyone was fooled. Even before the shuttle's first launch, in a prophetically titled cover story—"Beam Me Out of This Death Trap, Scotty"—for the *Washington Monthly* in 1980, Gregg Easterbrook compared the project with Howard

A Costly Enterprise

The average cost per launch was about $1.5 billion over the life of the US space-shuttle programme.

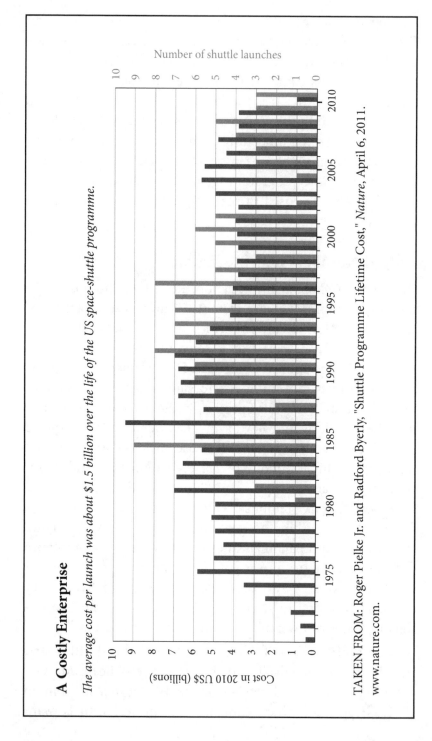

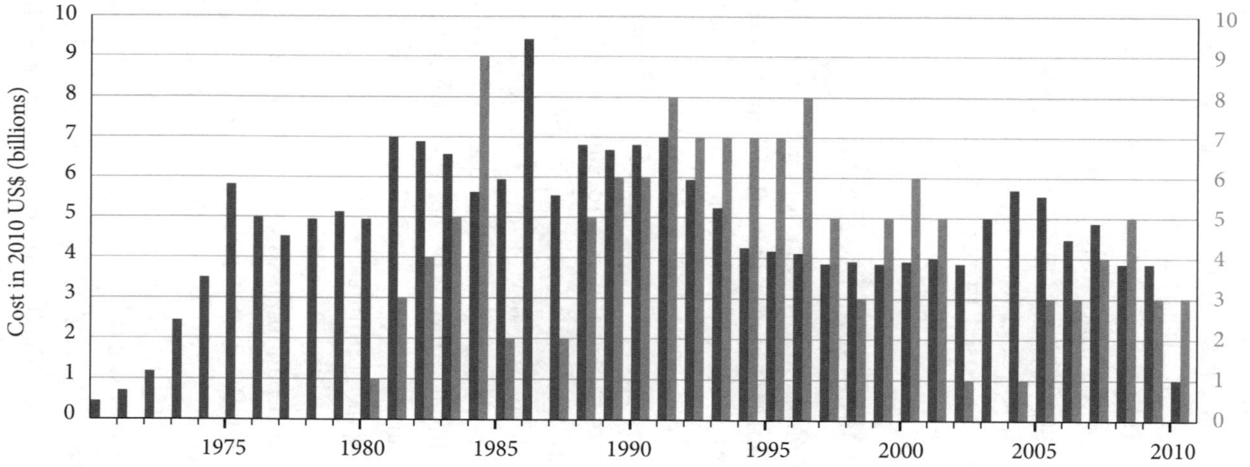

TAKEN FROM: Roger Pielke Jr. and Radford Byerly, "Shuttle Programme Lifetime Cost," *Nature*, April 6, 2011. www.nature.com.

Hughes's "Spruce Goose," the largest plane ever built, which managed to get only 70 feet off the ground in its sole flight. The magazine dubbed the shuttle program "Battlestar Bureauctica."

Investigating an agency that had already overspent its original budget and missed its forecasted launch date, Easterbrook found scientists seemingly disconnected from any sense of financial stewardship. Recalling the program's quest for cash in its early days, Jerry Gray, one of the original members of the shuttle technical team, used an equine metaphor: "First you have to get the horse," he told Easterbrook, "then you decide where to ride him." By 1980 the shuttle program had practically doubled its original budget; today, after three decades and almost $200 billion spent, it has missed almost every budget and performance goal.

The Problem with Mega Projects

Yet the shuttle program is just another entry in the ever-expanding file of large, ostensibly public projects that have lurched past deadlines and beyond financial limits. In their book *Megaprojects and Risk: An Anatomy of Ambition*, European planning and policy professors Bent Flyvbjerg, Nils Bruzelius, and Werner Rothengatter analyze dozens of public-works projects worldwide—from the "Chunnel" (the British Channel rail tunnel) to a high-speed rail project connecting Berlin and Hamburg to the construction of Denver International Airport. They draw some common lessons.

First, cost overruns are endemic to such massive projects. From the Chunnel, which nearly went bankrupt several times and exceeded original cost estimates by 80 percent, to Boston's "Big Dig" traffic tunnel upgrade, which ran 200 percent over budget, the impact on state and local coffers can be immense. Overall, the authors report that "the difference between actual and estimated investment cost is often 50–100 percent."

A second common thread in these ventures is that their advocates, eager to get them financed, vastly overstate projected public usage. Interestingly, this seems especially true of rail systems (both high-speed and standard urban rail) in comparison with road, bridge, and tunnel projects. While road infrastructure projects like the UK's Humber Bridge (which has seen just 25 percent of its forecast traffic) have underperformed, public rail projects have an especially poor track record when measured against original cost and usage estimates. Transportation secretary Ray LaHood, pushing ahead with a White House plan to build high-speed rail throughout the country, is either unaware of this research or unconvinced by it.

Explaining the Discrepancies

The *Megaprojects* authors find that blame for these fiascoes lies in a toxic pro-project mix of self-seeking "experts," politicians, and private-sector interests—combined with a minimum of public input. "It is easy to find motives for producing deceptive forecasts of costs and benefits," they write. "Politicians may have a 'monument complex,' engineers like to build things, and local officials sometimes have the mentality of empire builders. In addition, when a project goes forward, it creates work for engineers and construction firms, and many stakeholders make money." So while some might defend the errors as honest mistakes caused by unforeseen circumstances, the authors come to a more prosaic conclusion: "The use of deception and lying as tactics aimed at getting projects started appears to best explain why costs are highly and systematically underestimated and benefits overestimated in transport and infrastructure projects."

The authors' solution to the seemingly intractable problems of complex project construction is fairly straightforward: give taxpayers a say. They call for a "participatory and deliberative approach in including publics and stakeholders," which they argue will result in "decisions about risk that are better informed and more democratic." Encouragingly, more inclusive practices of this kind seem increasingly common around the world. From "citizen juries" and "public advisory councils" that oversee local development efforts in Europe and the United States to Stanford professor Jim Fishkin's "Deliberative Poll" methodology, which has been employed to plan public construction projects in China, citizens can and should take a larger role in decision making. Greater public participation will not only result in scuttling some unnecessary projects, but also prioritizing more urgent ones. As Flyvbjerg and his colleagues note, some meritorious projects never see the light of day because they lack the salesmanship and boosterism that have often supported expensive boondoggles.

During World War I, French prime minister Georges Clemenceau famously sniffed that "war is too important to be left to the military." In the same sense, as President Obama declares that "within 25 years, our goal is to give 80 percent of Americans access to high-speed rail," citizens should understand that such efforts are too important—and costly—to be left to engineers, politicians, and even rocket scientists.

VIEWPOINT 4

"Houston doesn't seek an orbiter because it wants to add a relic to a museum to highlight a marvel of modern engineering. It is more profound than that. To Houston and the men and women of Mission Control, who dedicated their careers to human spaceflight, it represents a life's work."

Houston Should Have Received a Retired Space Shuttle

Ted Poe and Pete Olson

Ted Poe and Pete Olson are Republican congressmen from Texas. In the following viewpoint, they criticize the decision not to give Houston a retired space shuttle, contending that no city in the world deserves one more. Poe and Olson point out that as the site of Mission Control, NASA has been an integral part of Houston for decades. They speculate that NASA's decision to exclude Houston is political in nature and demand answers from NASA administrator Charles Bolden.

Ted Poe and Pete Olson, "NASA, Houston Has a Problem," CNN.com, April 20, 2011.

As you read, consider the following questions:

1. Which four cities do the authors say are getting retired space shuttles?
2. How did the families of the astronauts who perished in the *Challenger* and *Columbia* missions react to news that Houston would not receive a retired space shuttle, according to the congressmen?
3. How many people do the authors say visit the Johnson Space Center in Houston every year?

Now that the space shuttle program is ending, no other place in the world deserves a retired shuttle more than Houston, Texas. Put simply, this decision should be a no-brainer.

But Houston has been overlooked. Shuttles are going to Los Angeles, Florida, and Washington. The prototype *Enterprise* is headed to New York City. "We were tremendously surprised," said Susan Marenoff-Zausner, president of the Intrepid Sea, Air and Space Museum in New York after NASA made the announcement. No kidding.

Sadly, it seems partisan politics permeates this announcement. And we are demanding answers.

Houston Is Space City, USA

The first word spoken on the moon landing was "Houston," not New York City. It defies logic for a shuttle not to land in "Space City, U.S.A." NASA has been ingrained in the culture of Houston for generations. The men and women who work at Mission Control in Houston have guided every single shuttle mission since the program began. Astronauts have raised their families in Houston. The families of the astronauts who perished in the *Challenger* and *Columbia* missions still live in Houston.

Senator John Cornyn's Statement on Retired Space Shuttle Decision

Like many Texans, I am disappointed with NASA's decision to slight the Johnson Space Center as a permanent home for one of the space shuttle orbiters. Houston has played a critical role throughout the life of the space shuttle, but it is clear political favors trumped common sense and fairness in the selection of the final locations for the orbiter fleet.

There is no question Houston should have been selected as a final home for one of the orbiters—even Administrator [Charles] Bolden stated as much. Today's announcement is an affront to the thousands of dedicated men and women at Johnson Space Center, the greater Houston community and the state of Texas, and I'm deeply disappointed with the administration's misguided decision.

John Cornyn,
"Cornyn Statement on Administration's Failure to Retire Orbiter to Rightful Home in Houston," April 12, 2011. http://cornyn.senate.gov.

The families said in a statement: "We again share a collective loss as a result of the political decision to send the space shuttle elsewhere." It is disrespectful to these heroes and their families not to bring a shuttle home to Houston in honor of those who paid the ultimate sacrifice for our nation's space program.

NASA administrator Charles Bolden justified his decision by saying that the locations he chose would give "the greatest number of people" the "best opportunity" to see the shuttles. He also cited access to national and international visitors.

Houston Deserves a Shuttle

Here's our justification for Houston: Houston is the fourth largest city in the United States, visited by nearly 7 million international visitors every year. More than 750,000 people a year visit the Johnson Space Center in Houston to glimpse the history of space exploration. Houston doesn't seek an orbiter because it wants to add a relic to a museum to highlight a marvel of modern engineering. It is more profound than that. To Houston and the men and women of Mission Control, who dedicated their careers to human spaceflight, it represents a life's work.

We can find no logical explanation for this mind-boggling decision. People from across America, including cities that also sought an orbiter, expressed disbelief that Houston would not receive a shuttle. This leads us to conclude that this administration allowed political favors to trump logic.

Calling NASA on the Carpet

The home of Mission Control deserves answers and that is why our Texas colleagues joined us in sending a letter to NASA administrator Charles Bolden asking him to explain his decision to Congress, the people of Houston and the American taxpayers.

NASA should be honest and provide the answers we seek on the criteria used to reach this decision and why Houston failed to meet those criteria. If, as we suspect, the measures were purely political, we will do everything in our power to make this right.

Above all else, NASA is an agency that has always served above politics, and the amazing people who work at the Johnson Space Center have always risen to every challenge presented to them. They deserve answers.

Viewpoint 5

"Houston didn't get an orbiter because nobody outside of the JSC [Johnson Space Center] area cared."

There Are Good Reasons Houston Did Not Get a Retired Space Shuttle

Michael Grabois

Michael Grabois has worked on the space shuttle for NASA contractors for twenty years. In the following viewpoint, he asserts that the reason Houston did not get a retired space shuttle might be because they did not put in a better bid than the cities that did get one. Grabois also points out that the poor way Space Center Houston displays its already-existing spaceflight hardware may also have been an influence on the decision. It is possible, he argues, that the decision had nothing to do with politics and everything to do with how far Houston was willing to go to procure a shuttle.

As you read, consider the following questions:

1. Why would Barack Obama want to punish Texas by denying them a retired space shuttle, according to the author?

Michael Grabois, "Don't Blame NASA or Politics for an Orbiter-less Houston," *Houston Chronicle*, April 15, 2011. Reproduced by permission of the author.

2. What two factors does the author cite as crucial to a winning bid?
3. According to Grabois, what did the city of Houston do to woo the decision makers?

It's easy to look at NASA awarding the soon-to-be-retired space shuttles to places other than Houston, home of the Johnson Space Center [JSC], in purely political terms. After all, hasn't the president [Barack Obama] shown contempt for the state of Texas in the past? Isn't Texas a "red state", and didn't the president lose here twice in 2008 (first to Hillary Clinton in the primary, then to the Republicans in the national election)? Isn't this just another example of how politicized everything is, that he took the opportunity to thumb his nose at us? Well, maybe. But if you can look past the politics just for a moment, there are several good reasons why NASA may have done what it did. There's a lot of speculation in here—I have no knowledge whatsoever of the bid process, I haven't seen any of the bids, and I haven't talked to anyone else involved—but no wild leaps to unfounded conclusions.

Before going further, let me state that I've been working on the space shuttle for NASA contractors in Houston for over 20 years, my entire adult life. This commentary, however, is completely my own thoughts and speculations and does not represent the views of my employers. I'm speaking here as an individual, a Houstonian, a taxpayer, a rocket scientist.

I was out at two NASA-related events on Tuesday night. Of course, the main topic of conversation was that not only did NASA HQ [headquarters] slap JSC in the face by not giving us an orbiter, but they added insult to injury by only giving us a pair of used space shuttle seats. I was as mad as the next guy until I heard multiple people at both parties discussing possible reasons why. The general consensus was that NASA didn't screw over JSC and Houston, you have to blame

Space Center Houston and the city of Houston itself instead. Here's why—and it's totally free of politics.

Strike 1: When it's all done, the simulators and orbiters are no more than excess government property, though special property designated for museums. And because there are only a limited number of these pieces, there has to be a way to be "fair" in awarding them, so it's up to the museums to submit the best bid. If a museum wants something, it puts in a bid in accordance with the published rules. If Houston did not get an orbiter, it's because the Space Center Houston bid was not considered good enough. That includes two important factors: facilities and tourism. With limited number of other space artifacts to be distributed (engines, simulators, mockups, etc.), according to the rules made available at the time, the museum had to bid on those too. If Houston did not get a simulator, it's because either the Space Center Houston bid was subpar or they didn't bid on the item at all. See a pattern developing here? Maybe someone assumed that Houston would automatically get something because it's right next to JSC. But Space Center Houston is a separate entity that does not automatically get JSC's hand-me-downs. How bad could their bid have been that they didn't get anything except a pair of seats?

A recent article in the *Chronicle* says "The space agency opted to place the shuttles in locations . . . where it believes the greatest number of people could see the spacecraft." Admittedly, New York City and Los Angeles each get more tourists than Houston does. But Senator [Kay Bailey] Hutchison is also quoted as saying "priority should be given to communities with strong historical ties to NASA, and in particular the shuttle program." If the rule was that number of tourists was a higher priority than historical ties, then Houston never had a chance. The fact that the California Science Center ". . . hasn't hired an architect yet to design the new facility and is now planning a fund-raiser" should say something about how tourism trumped historical ties.

NASA Administrator Charles Bolden's Announcement About Retired Space Shuttles

Today, I am proud to announce where these national treasures will be displayed and enjoyed by millions of Americans, once the shuttle program concludes.

First, here at the Kennedy Space Center, where every shuttle mission and so many other historic human spaceflights have originated, we'll showcase my old friend *Atlantis*, right here behind us. Not only will the workers who sent it into space so many times have a chance to still see it, the thousands of visitors who come here every year to learn more about space and to be a part of the excitement of exploration will be able to see what is still a great rarity, an actual space-flown vehicle.

The California Science Center in Los Angeles—only a few miles from the site of the old Rockwell plant where the shuttle was developed and from where its construction was managed—will be the new home of the shuttle on the launch pad preparing for its final mission—*Endeavour*.

The Smithsonian's National Air and Space Museum Steven F. Udvar-Hazy Center in Virginia will get *Discovery*, our most-traveled orbiter.

And New York City's Intrepid Sea, Air and Space Museum—on whose flight deck Mercury and Gemini modules and flight crews were returned to us after splash down from their historic space missions—will get *Enterprise*, our prototype orbiter that tested the aerodynamics of the craft before it flew into space.

Charles Bolden,
"Remarks for Administrator Bolden at the 30th Anniversary of STS-1," April 12, 2011.

Strike 2: Part of the decision on who got an orbiter was dependent on how much the home city was involved in the promotion, from drumming up interest and creating a website to the number of visitors the museum gets to how involved the city and its politicians are. Look at New York's Intrepid [Sea, Air and Space] Museum—they had been very publicly chasing an orbiter for years, with rallies, parties, senators and congressmen, the works. What had the city of Houston done? There's a website that I heard about for the first time earlier this year, and they held a rally a couple weeks ago. If NY Senators [Charles E.] Schumer and [Kristen] Gillibrand and Mayor [Michael] Bloomberg could stump for their city, where were Senators Hutchison and [John] Cornyn during this time? Where was Mayor [Annise] Parker? Where was [Representative] Sheila Jackson Lee, who never met a TV camera she didn't like? Houston didn't get an orbiter because nobody outside of the JSC area cared. I'm not the only one to say this, read this recent essay by former shuttle flight director and shuttle program manager Wayne Hale: "Houston didn't get an orbiter because Houston didn't deserve it."

Strike 3: Last but not least, look at how Space Center Houston displays its already-existing spaceflight hardware. The last major artifact to be put (back) on display was the restored Saturn V, which used to sit outside in the elements until a restoration was performed. While the conservators did an outstanding job on the restoration, someone did a lousy job on the building that houses it. It's little more than a corrugated tin shack. . . . If a new, better, more permanent building was to be constructed after the restoration, well, it's been years already. Outside of the rocket itself, the only other things in the building are a wall panel for each of the Apollo missions containing a crew photo, a patch, and a description of the mission. There are far more artifacts and things to do inside the Saturn V pavilion at the Kennedy Space Center in Florida—there's a moon rock, interactive exhibits, and more. Space

Center Houston practically hides the Mercury, Gemini, and Apollo capsules; the Starship Gallery can only be reached after sitting through a presentation or by going around it, behind some kiddie exhibits. These are priceless relics of the early space race and they're essentially hidden. Houston didn't get an orbiter because the evaluation team probably didn't like how Space Center Houston already displays their space relics.

There. I've laid out what I think is a good, logical, nonpartisan explanation for why Houston didn't get an orbiter or any other simulator. They got what they asked for (two seats) and didn't get whatever else they may have asked for because they were outbid and out-presented. And that doesn't even take into account any hypothetical political pressure, but with 3 strikes against it, politics may not have even needed to have been a consideration. Of course, political opportunists will always inject politics to suit their own purposes anyway.

Periodical and Internet Sources Bibliography

The following articles have been selected to supplement the diverse views presented in this chapter.

Chloe Albanesius	"Bill Would Give Space Shuttle to Texas, Not New York," *PC Magazine*, April 15, 2011.
Eric Berger	"Houston, We've Had a Problem: 'Space City' Snubbed in Bid for Retired Space Shuttle," *SciGuy* (blog), *Houston Chronicle*, April 12, 2011. http://blog.chron.com/sciguy.
Rebecca Boyle	"Florida, California, Washington D.C. and New York City to Receive Retired Space Shuttles," *Popular Science*, April 12, 2011.
Chris Carroll	"End of Shuttle Leaves Future of Manned Spaceflight Unclear," *Stars and Stripes*, July 6, 2011.
Tony Dokoupil	"The Next Space Race," *Newsweek*, July 11, 2011.
David Roth	"Transcendence Splashes Down," *New York*, April 24, 2011.
Mike Schneider	"NASA Grants Intrepid Museum Retired Space Shuttles," *Huffington Post*, April 12, 2011.
Tindel	"Why Houston Should Not Get a Space Shuttle," *The Space Geek*, April 23, 2011. www.thespacegeek.com.
John Noble Wilford	"3, 2, 1, and the Last Shuttle Leaves an Era Behind," *New York Times*, July 8, 2011.
John Zarrella	"Astronauts Ponder Future as Shuttle Program Winds Down," CNN.com, April 28, 2011. www.cnn.com.

OPPOSING VIEWPOINTS® SERIES

CHAPTER 3

How Should NASA Be Funded?

Chapter Preface

On February 1, 2010, President Barack Obama released his 2011 National Aeronautics and Space Administration (NASA) budget, an appropriation of $19 billion. During the announcement, he outlined NASA's goals in the near term: "we will ramp up robotic exploration of the solar system, including a probe of the sun's atmosphere; new scouting missions to Mars and other destinations; and an advanced telescope to follow Hubble, helping us to protect our environment for future generations. We will increase Earth-based observation to improve our understanding of our climate and our world—science that will garner tangible benefits, helping us to protect our environment for future generations. And we will extend the life of the International Space Station likely by more than five years, while actually using it for its intended purpose: conducting advanced research that can help the daily lives of people here on Earth, as well as testing and improving upon our capabilities in space."

Obama's NASA budget immediately generated controversy. Critics noted that the administration was effectively killing the Constellation program, which planned for a manned mission to the moon by 2020. It also eliminated the Ares I rocket, which was regarded as the successor to the space shuttle. Critics accused Obama's budget of being a disaster for human spaceflight and for America's reputation as an undisputed leader in space. Former NASA administrator Michael Griffin argued that the budget "means that essentially the U.S. has decided that they're not going to be a significant player in human spaceflight for the foreseeable future."

Another controversy was the budget's emphasis of the private sector and its expanded role in space transportation and exploration. In Obama's budget, he called for spending $6 billion over five years to develop a commercial spacecraft that could taxi astronauts to and from the International Space Station. Critics attacked the idea of greater private-sector involvement, arguing that private industry was not ready to take over vital space-related tasks, projects, and missions. Others maintain that space exploration and settlement should be a government activity, not left to private industries who value profit above all else.

Obama defended the decision to rely more on the private sector for some aspects of space exploration and transportation. "The truth is, NASA has always relied on private industry to help design and build the vehicles that carry the astronauts to space, from the Mercury capsule that carried John Glenn into orbit nearly 50 years ago, to the space shuttle *Discovery* currently orbiting overhead," he said at the budget announcement. "By buying the services of space transportation—rather than the vehicles themselves—we can continue to ensure rigorous safety standards are met. But we will also accelerate the pace of innovations of companies—from young start-ups to established leaders—compete to design and build and launch new means of carrying people and materials out of our atmosphere."

The controversy over the NASA budget is one of the issues explored in the following chapter. Other viewpoints examine the role of private industry in space development and exploration and the funding for NASA education programs.

VIEWPOINT 1

> *"In essence, the new spending plan takes NASA back to its roots of advanced technology development, experimentation and exploration."*

President Obama's NASA Budget Should Be Approved

Newt Gingrich and Robert S. Walker

Newt Gingrich is former Speaker of the House of Representatives and is on the board of governors of the National Space Society. Robert S. Walker was chairman of the Commission on the Future of the United States Aerospace Industry. In the following viewpoint, they contend that the Obama administration's NASA budget deserves strong approval from both Republicans and Democrats. Gingrich and Walker argue that the new budget adheres to what experts and presidential commissions have been recommending for a decade. They also note that it makes some tough choices that will free up funds to pursue some essential advanced technology development that will have long-range benefits for the United States.

Newt Gingrich and Robert S. Walker, "Obama's Brave Reboot for NASA," *Washington Times*, February 12, 2010.

As you read, consider the following questions:

1. What did the Commission on the Future of the United States Aerospace Industry suggest in 2002?
2. What do the authors cite as the reason for the termination of the Constellation program?
3. According to the authors, what are the benefits of US reliance on commercial launch services?

Despite the shrieks you might have heard from a few special interests, the [Barack] Obama administration's budget for the National Aeronautics and Space Administration deserves strong approval from Republicans. The 2011 spending plan for the space agency does what is obvious to anyone who cares about man's future in space and what presidential commissions have been recommending for nearly a decade.

The Commission on the Future of the United States Aerospace Industry in 2002 suggested that greater commercial activity in space was the proper way forward. The Aldridge Commission of 2004, headed by former Secretary of the Air Force Edward C. "Pete" Aldridge, made clear that the only way NASA could achieve success with President George W. Bush's Vision for Space Exploration was to expand the space enterprise with greater use of commercial assets. Most recently, the Augustine Commission, headed by Norman R. Augustine, former chief executive of Lockheed Martin, made clear that commercial providers of space-launch services were a necessary part of maintaining space leadership for the United States.

NASA consistently ignored or rejected the advice provided to it by outside experts. The internal culture within the agency was actively hostile to commercial enterprise. A belief had grown from the days when the Apollo program landed humans on the moon that only NASA could do space well and therefore only NASA projects and programs were worthy. To his credit, former NASA Administrator Michael Griffin adopted a program to begin to access commercial companies for hauling cargo to the International Space Station. That program existed alongside the much larger effort to build a new generation of space vehicles designed to take us back to the moon. It has been under constant financial pressure because of the cost overruns in the moon mission, called Constellation.

With the new NASA budget, the leadership of the agency is attempting to refocus the manned space program along the lines that successive panels of experts have recommended. The space shuttle program, which was scheduled to end, largely for safety reasons, will be terminated as scheduled. The Constellation program also will be terminated, mostly because its ongoing costs cannot be absorbed within projected NASA budget limits. The International Space Station will have its life extended to at least 2020, thereby preserving a $100 billion laboratory asset that otherwise was due to be dumped in the Pacific Ocean by mid-decade. The budget also sets forth an aggressive program for having cargo and astronaut crews delivered to the space station by commercial providers.

The use of commercial launch companies to carry cargo and crews into low-earth orbit will be controversial, but it should not be. The launch-vehicle portion of the Constellation program was so far behind schedule that the United States was not going to have independent access for humans into space for at least five years after the shutdown of the shuttle. We were going to rely upon the Russians to deliver our astronaut personnel to orbit. We have long had a cooperative arrangement with the Russians for space transportation but always have possessed our own capability. The use of commercial carriers in the years ahead will preserve that kind of independent American access.

Reliance on commercial launch services will provide many other benefits. It will open the doors to more people having the opportunity to go to space. It has the potential of creating thousands of new jobs, largely the kind of high-tech work to which our nation should aspire. In the same way the railroads opened the American West, commercial access can open vast new opportunities in space. All of this new activity will expand the space enterprise, and in doing so, will improve the economic competitiveness of our country.

Critics likely will raise the issue of safety and reliability. However, there already are rockets in the American inventory that are trusted by our government to launch billion-dollar satellites and have proved to be quite reliable. Those vehicles can be modified to carry human crews safely. New rockets under development have been designed from the outset with manned missions in mind, and with the assurance of NASA business, necessary large-scale development can be done so they can be added to the commercial inventory. The plan is to have both NASA and the Federal Aviation Administration provide licensing oversight, determine safety requirements and approve all launches.

But the ambition of the NASA leadership is much larger. Getting the agency out of the low-earth-orbit launch business frees up the budget to do other exciting and valuable things. It permits development work to start in earnest on a heavy-lift launch vehicle capable of solar-system exploration. It enables expansion of the aeronautics budget, particularly in helping develop the next-generation air-traffic-control system, a technological goal that will pay huge dividends to the United States. It will permit new investments in robotic space missions and Earth science missions. In essence, the new spending plan takes NASA back to its roots of advanced technology development, experimentation and exploration.

Bipartisan cooperation has been difficult to achieve in Congress, but here is a chance. By looking forward, NASA has given us a way to move forward. It deserves broad support for daring to challenge the status quo. It has proposed the real change that Americans are seeking.

Viewpoint 2

> *"We must not allow the president to neuter our space program."*

President Obama's NASA Budget Should Not Be Approved

George Landrith

George Landrith is president of the Frontiers of Freedom Institute. In the following viewpoint, he disparages the Obama administration's NASA budget, arguing that it effectively prioritizes public relations and researching climate change over space exploration. Landrith urges Congress to force revisions of the NASA budget to fund another moon landing and, eventually, a manned trip to Mars. He contends that if the United States doesn't continue to pursue these ambitious missions, other countries will.

As you read, consider the following questions:

1. According to the author, what did NASA administrator Charles Bolden reveal about one of President Obama's primary missions for NASA?
2. What are three common products the author says were a creation of the space program?

George Landrith, "America Belongs in Space," *Human Events*, November 28, 2010.

3. How much money does NASA spend per year, according to the author?

NASA has been in the news for all the wrong reasons the past twelve months. First, the White House reportedly directed NASA to concentrate on Earth-based projects like researching climate change rather than returning to the moon, reestablishing U.S. space dominance, or exploring Mars. Second, [President Barack] Obama's NASA administrator Charles Bolden revealed that one of President Obama's primary missions for NASA was to "reach out to the Muslim world" to help Islamic nations "feel good" about their contributions and accomplishments in the scientific arena. In other words, NASA will become an international feel-good organization.

Some might argue that in financially tight times, it is necessary to cut spending and thus kill planned missions to the moon and to Mars. But NASA's budget hasn't been cut—only its mission has been gutted and its vision clouded. That is a HUGE mistake.

NASA's Priorities

NASA should be working to keep the United States as the world leader in space exploration. There are billions of dollars spent on climate research, and NASA doesn't need to duplicate those efforts. And the idea of making NASA an international counseling organization to help Islamic nations feel better about their lack of high-technology development is utterly silly.

Since the last Apollo mission in the 1970s, our space exploration program has focused on low-Earth orbit. The United States needs to get back into the business of looking farther into outer space. We need to develop a heavy-lift launch capability. But NASA cannot do this job if the president's foresight is so weak and unimaginative. President John F. Kennedy focused the nation on a bold vision that captured the American imagination. Obama would do well to follow his example.

Obama Administration Budget Puts America at Risk

The president's plan only ensures that for decades to come the United States will be both subservient to, and reliant on, other countries for our access to space. Future generations will learn how the Chinese, the Russians, and even the Indians took the reins of human space exploration away from the United States.

This request abandons our nation's only chance to remain the leader in space and instead chooses to set up a welfare program for the commercial space industry. It is a plan where the taxpayer subsidizes billionaires to build rockets that NASA hopes one day will allow millionaires, and our own astronauts, to travel to space.

Richard Shelby, Statement of Senator Richard C. Shelby before the Commerce, Justice, Science and Related Agencies Appropriations Subcommittee, April 22, 2010. http://shelby.senate.gov.

A Failure of Vision

A failure of vision has real costs. Much of the advancement and growth in the economy the past three decades have their roots in the space program. Transistors, circuit boards, computerization and miniaturization technologies were all advanced at unprecedented rates by the space program, not to mention the marketability of Tang or Ziploc bags. Ask yourself, what would have happened had Queen Isabella turned Christopher Columbus down and refused to fund exploration to find alternative trade routes to the East? What would have happened if Sir Francis Drake or Ferdinand Magellan had not been sent out to explore? What if President Thomas Jefferson had decided to save money rather than to send [Meriwether] Lewis and [William] Clark out to explore and chart North America?

NASA doesn't spend much money—a paltry $18 billion—but how that money is spent matters a great deal! Will it be spent to counsel Muslims who feel sad that they haven't landed on the moon? Will it be spent to duplicate the billions already spent on climate research? Or will it be spent to explore the frontiers of space? Will it be spent doing amazing and inspiring things, or wasted doing mundane and unimportant things?

Let NASA Be NASA

It is time for NASA to again be in the big-vision business. We need to head back to the moon so that we can hone our skills and technology for the more demanding trip to Mars and other yet unknown challenges. That means we need to develop a heavy-lift rocket and a space vehicle that can safely carry astronauts into deep space and bring them home again. Each year we wait means time lost toward achieving those goals. Even worse, as we delay and waste time, our space and high-tech industries shrink, and we slowly become less capable of accomplishing myriad goals. If the president lacks the vision to direct NASA to perform its natural function, Congress should intervene and push the point. We must not allow the president to neuter our space program. Other nations with less myopic leadership will quickly fill the void, leaving the United States to play catch-up for decades to come.

Americans are by their very nature explorers. This country was founded by explorers. In our nation's early history, we explored the western frontiers. More recently, we led the way in space exploration. As a boy, I grew up admiring John Glenn, Neil Armstrong, Buzz Aldrin, and Jim Lovell. I watched with amazement as men walked on the moon and planted the American flag there. I watched the space shuttle fly off into the sky and become the backbone of a vibrant space-station program. There is value in being inspired by great visions and amazing accomplishments. Our children ought to have the chance to reach for the stars. We ought not to dream small dreams; small dreams do not inspire or motivate. We ought not to limit our children's hope or vision.

Viewpoint 3

> *"Finding a political middle that can support NASA's program through many presidencies would be Obama's biggest legacy in space."*

The United States Must Provide Stable Funding for the Space Program

Christian Science Monitor

The Christian Science Monitor *is a daily international newspaper. In the following viewpoint, the editorial board maintains that congressional opposition to the Barack Obama administration's NASA budget forced the president to reconfigure NASA priorities, which now include a schedule for a human spaceflight to Mars. The president must continue to work with Congress to establish a system of stable funding for NASA that can withstand partisan bickering and maneuvering. This is key to cementing American leadership in space.*

As you read, consider the following questions:

1. What year do the authors say NASA has scheduled a trip to land on an asteroid?

"NASA and Obama's Budget: The Politics and Ideals of Human Space Exploration," Reproduced by permission from the April 16, 2010, issue of *The Christian Science Monitor*.

2. According to the authors, the Obama budget plans to raise NASA's overall budget by how much?

3. What do the authors think President Obama relied on too much in his budget plan for NASA?

Human travel to Mars is now back on America's space agenda.

It is just one of many course-corrections that President [Barack] Obama will likely be forced to make to his January [2010] proposals for big changes at NASA.

A Compromise on NASA Budget

Too many Americans and lawmakers reacted negatively to the initial White House plan for the National Aeronautics and Space Administration [NASA]. They still see human exploration to specific destinations in space as a compelling frontier—not just for the nation but humanity, too. They weren't ready to live only vague promises of deep-space missions, as Mr. Obama made. Nor do they want the space agency more focused on earthly tasks such as climate change monitoring, as Obama would prefer, over scientific discovery in outer space.

The public reaction pushed the president on Thursday [April 15, 2010] to set a timetable for the first Mars trip—by the mid-2030s—as well as a schedule to land on an asteroid (near 2025). He also had to set 2015 for starting construction of a heavy-lift launcher based on new innovative technology.

America's Space Leadership

But Obama only partially backed down on his proposal to cancel a [George W.] Bush-era program called Constellation. That project, now over budget, would return Americans to the moon to do more research and to tap that body's frozen water for making fuel for lunar launches to Mars and beyond. While he still wants to stop production of the Ares rockets for the moon mission, Obama did backpedal a bit by offering to keep

NASA Dollars Boost the Economies of Every State in the United States

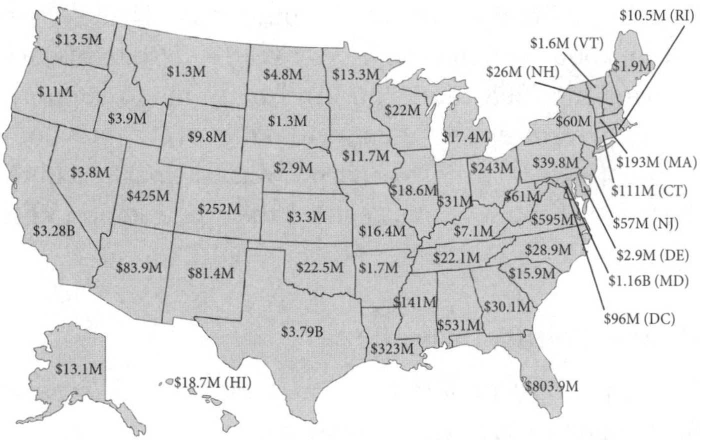

All 50 states and the District of Columbia participated in NASA procurements in FY '03

Grants and awards went to various educational institutions and nonprofit organizations in 50 states and the District of Columbia

TAKEN FROM: NASA Procurement Management Service Online Query Web Page. http://prod.nais.nasa.gov/cgi-bin/npms/map.cgi.

the planned Orion crew-ship—but only as an emergency vehicle to escape the International Space Station.

Even Neil Armstrong, the first human on the moon, opposes an end to the moon project, partly because other nations, especially China, are gearing up to land there in the years ahead. America's leadership in space would be in jeopardy.

The Battle in Congress

The political battle over funding the moon project will play out in Congress over coming months. Some compromise may be possible. This debate will likely have little of the polarizing partisan tones of other issues on Capitol Hill. Rather, it pits key political states with many space-related jobs—Florida, Texas, California, and Colorado—against other states.

To his credit, the president would raise NASA's overall budget by about $6 billion over five years—despite his call for cuts during his 2008 campaign. And he wants to support the fledgling private space agency to take over many of the government's goals for low-orbit projects, such as reaching the space station. He also would extend the space station's life by four years.

Finding a Political Middle

Finding a political middle that can support NASA's program through many presidencies would be Obama's biggest legacy in space. The agency and the private contractors can keep suffering financial whiplash every few years, as they did once again when Obama laid out his goals last January.

One of those potential middle positions was articulated well by Obama on Thursday: "Our goal is the capacity for people to work and learn, operate and live safely beyond the Earth for extended periods of time."

The president erred by not working more closely with Congress before setting forth his budget plan for NASA. He also may be counting too much on the commercial space-launch industry to mature soon enough to take over key NASA functions and fill the gap—to be temporarily filled by Russian rockets—caused by the end of the space shuttle program this fall.

He's on course, however, when he clearly lines himself up with America's strong tradition in spaceflight, as he did Thursday in speaking at the Kennedy Space Center:

"Space exploration is not a luxury, not an afterthought in America's brighter future, [but] an essential part of that quest. . . . For pennies on the dollar, the space program has improved our lives, advanced our society, strengthened our economy, and inspired generations."

VIEWPOINT 4

> *"At its core, NASA's mission remains fundamentally the same as it always has been and supports our new vision: 'To reach for new heights and reveal the unknown so that what we do and learn will benefit all humankind.'"*

NASA Must Make Tough Funding Choices

Charles F. Bolden Jr.

Charles F. Bolden Jr. is the NASA administrator. In the following viewpoint, he states that the Barack Obama administration's budget makes tough choices and will enable NASA to meet the challenges of the twenty-first century. Bolden argues that NASA's focus is on an ambitious path of innovation and technical advancement that will improve human life and expand US presence in space for knowledge and commerce. One of NASA's key goals is also economic, with an emphasis on supporting long-term job growth and economic competitiveness and cementing America's role as technology leader.

As you read, consider the following questions:

1. How much is the 2012 budget request for NASA?

Charles F. Bolden Jr., Statement before the Senate Committee on Commerce, Science, and Transportation, March 15, 2011.

2. What American president does Bolden identify as the one who set the United States on a path of unprecedented achievement in space?

3. According to Bolden, what is the role of NASA's Aeronautics Research Mission Directorate (ARMD)?

The president's [Barack Obama's] FY [fiscal year] 2012 budget request of $18.7 billion for NASA continues the agency's focus on a reinvigorated path of innovation and technological discovery leading to an array of challenging destinations and missions that increases our knowledge, develops technologies to improve life, [and] expands our presence in space for knowledge and commerce and that will engage the public. With the president's signing of the NASA Authorization Act of 2010 (P.L. 111-267) on October 11, 2010, NASA has a clear direction and is moving forward. NASA appreciates the significant effort that advanced this important bipartisan legislation, particularly efforts by the leadership and members of this committee [Senate Committee on Commerce, Science, and Transportation]. This is a time of opportunity for NASA to shape a promising future for the nation's space program.

Because these are tough fiscal times, tough choices had to be made. But the proposed FY 2012 budget funds all major elements of the Authorization Act, supporting a diverse portfolio of programs, while making difficult choices to fund key priorities and reduce other areas in order to invest in the future. . . .

NASA Priorities

We have an incredible balance of human spaceflight, science, aeronautics and technology development. Within the human spaceflight arena, our foremost priority is our current human spaceflight endeavor—the International Space Station [ISS]—and the safety and viability of the astronauts aboard it. The request also maintains a strong commitment to human spaceflight beyond low-Earth orbit [LEO]. It establishes critical priorities and invests in the technologies and excellent science, aeronautics research, and education programs that will help us win the future. The request supports an aggressive launch rate over the next two years with about 40 US and international missions to the ISS, for science, and to support other agencies.

At its core, NASA's mission remains fundamentally the same as it always has been and supports our new vision: "To reach for new heights and reveal the unknown so that what we do and learn will benefit all humankind." This statement is from the new multi-year 2011 NASA Strategic Plan accompanying the FY 2012 budget request, which all of NASA's mission directorates, mission support offices and centers helped to develop, and encapsulates in broad terms the very reason for NASA's existence and everything that the American public expects from its space program. Just last week, we completed the space shuttle *Discovery*'s STS-133 mission, one of the final three shuttle flights to the International Space Station. *Discovery* delivered a robotic crew member, Robonaut 2 (R2), and supplies that will support the station's scientific research and technology demonstrations. We recently made some preliminary announcements about program offices to carry out our future work. And we plan to release three additional high-priority solicitations spanning Space Technology's strategic investment areas. NASA brings good jobs and bolsters the economy in communities across the nation. Our space program continues to venture in ways that will have long-term benefits, and there are many more milestones in the very near term.

Human Spaceflight Priorities

Our human spaceflight priorities in the FY 2012 budget request are to:

- safely fly the last space shuttle flights this year and maintain safe access for humans to low-Earth orbit as we fully utilize the International Space Station;
- facilitate safe, reliable, and cost-effective U.S.-provided commercial access to low-Earth orbit first for cargo and then for crew as quickly as possible;
- begin to lay the groundwork for expanding human presence into deep space—the moon, asteroids, eventually Mars—through development of a powerful heavy-lift rocket and multi-purpose crew capsule; and
- pursue technology development that is needed to carry humans farther into the solar system. Taken together, these human spaceflight initiatives will enable America to retain its position as a leader in space exploration for generations to come.

At the same time, we will extend our reach with robots and scientific observatories to expand our knowledge of the universe beyond our own planet. We will continue the vital work to expand our abilities to observe our planet Earth and make that data available for decision makers. We will also continue our groundbreaking research into the next generation of aviation technologies. Finally, we will make the most of all of NASA's technological breakthroughs to improve life here at home.

With the FY 2012 budget, NASA will carry out research, technology and innovation programs that support long-term job growth and economic competitiveness and build upon our nation's position as a technology leader. We will educate the next generation of technology leaders through vital programs in science, technology, engineering, and mathematics education. And we will build the future through those investments in American industry to create a new job-producing engine for the U.S. economy.

The Kennedy Legacy

This year we honor the legacy of President John F. Kennedy, who 50 years ago, set the United States on a path that resulted in a national effort to produce an unprecedented achievement. Now, we step forward along a similar path, engaged in a wide range of activities in human spaceflight, technology development, science, and aeronautics—a path characterized by engagement of an expanded commercial space sector and technology development to mature the capabilities required by increasingly challenging missions designed to make discoveries and reach new destinations.

NASA's Science Mission Directorate (SMD) continues to rewrite textbooks and make headlines around the world. Across disciplines and geographic regions worldwide, NASA aims to achieve a deep scientific understanding of Earth, other planets and solar system bodies, our star system in its entirety, and the universe beyond. The agency is laying the foundation for the robotic and human expeditions of the future while meeting today's needs for scientific information to address national concerns about global change, space weather, and education.

- The Mars Science Laboratory will launch later this year and arrive at Mars in August 2012. It will be the largest rover ever to reach the Red Planet and will search for evidence of both past and present life.
- The Nuclear Spectroscopic Telescope Array (NuSTAR) mission will launch in early 2012 and become the first focusing hard X-ray telescope to orbit Earth.
- Research and analysis programs will use data from an array of sources, including spacecraft, sounding rockets, balloons, and payloads on the ISS. We will continue to evaluate the vast amounts of data we receive from dozens of ongoing missions supported by this budget.

- A continued focus on Earth Science sees us continuing development of the Orbiting Carbon Observatory-2 (OCO-2) for launch in 2013 and other initiatives to collect data about our home planet across the spectrum.
- The budget reflects the scientific priorities for astrophysics as expressed in the recent decadal survey of the National Academy of Sciences. The budget supports small-, medium-, and large-scale activities recommended by the decadal survey.
- The Radiation Belt Storm Probe mission will launch next year, and development of other smaller missions and instruments to study the sun will get under way here on the ground.

With the appointment of a new chief scientist, NASA will pursue an integrated, strategic approach to its scientific work across mission directorates and programs.

More NASA Goals

As we continue our work to consolidate the Exploration Systems and Space Operations Mission Directorates (ESMD and SOMD), both groups will support our current human spaceflight programs and continue work on technologies to expand our future capabilities.

- We will fly out the space shuttle in 2011, including STS-135 if funds are available, and then proceed with the disposition of most space shuttle assets after the retirement of the fleet. The shuttle program accomplished many outstanding things for this nation, and in 2012 we look forward to moving our retired orbiters to museums and science centers across the country to inspire the next generation of explorers.

- Completing assembly of the U.S. segment of the ISS will be the crowning achievement of the space shuttle's nearly 30-year history. The ISS will serve as a fully functional and permanently crewed research laboratory and technology test bed, providing a critical stepping stone for exploration and future international cooperation, as well as an invaluable national laboratory for non-NASA and nongovernmental users. During FY 2011, NASA will award a cooperative agreement to an independent nonprofit organization (NPO) with responsibility to further develop national uses of the ISS. The NPO will oversee all ISS research involving organizations other than NASA, and transfer current NASA biological and physical research to the NPO in future years.
- In 2012, we will make progress in developing a new Space Launch System (SLS), a heavy-lift rocket that will be the first step on our eventual journeys to destinations beyond LEO.
- We will continue work on a Multi-Purpose Crew Vehicle (MPCV) that will build on the human safety features, designs, and systems of the Orion Crew Exploration Vehicle. As with the SLS, acquisition strategy decisions will be finalized by this summer.
- NASA will continue to expand commercial access to space and work with our partners to achieve milestones in the Commercial Orbital Transportation Services (COTS) program, the Commercial Resupply Services (CRS) effort, and an expanded Commercial Crew Development (CCDev) program. As we direct resources toward developing these capabilities, we not only create multiple means for accessing LEO, we also facilitate commercial uses of space, help lower costs, and spark

an engine for long-term job growth. While the request is above the authorized level for 2012, NASA believes the amount is critical, combined with significant corporate investments, to ensure that we will have one or more companies that can transport American astronauts to the ISS. With retirement of the space shuttle in 2011, this is a top agency priority.

- Most importantly, NASA recognizes that these programmatic changes will continue to personally affect thousands of NASA civil servants and contractors who have worked countless hours, often under difficult circumstances, to make our human spaceflight, science, and aeronautics programs and projects successful. I commend the investment that these dedicated Americans have made and will continue to make in our nation's space and aeronautics programs. These are tremendously exciting and dynamic times for the U.S. space program. NASA will strive to utilize our workforce in a manner that will ensure that the nation maintains NASA's greatest asset—the skilled civil servants and contractors—while working to increase the efficiency and cost-effectiveness in all of its operations.
- The 21st Century Space Launch Complex [21st CSLC] program will focus on upgrades to the Florida launch range, expanding capabilities to support SLS, MPCV, commercial cargo/launch services providers, and transforming KSC [Kennedy Space Center] into a modern facility that benefits all range users. The program will replan its activities based on available FY 2011 funding to align with 2010 NASA Authorization's focus areas, including cross organizational coordination between 21st CSLC, launch services, and commercial crew activities.

Improving Air Travel

NASA's Aeronautics Research Mission Directorate (ARMD) continues to improve the safety, efficiency and environmental friendliness of air travel.

- Our work continues to address the challenge of meeting the growing technology and capacity needs of the next generation air travel system, or "NextGen," in coordination with the FAA [Federal Aviation Administration] and other stakeholders in airspace efficiency.
- NASA's work on green aviation technologies that improve fuel efficiency and reduce noise continues apace.
- We also continue to work . . . to develop the concepts and technologies for the aircraft of tomorrow. The agency's fundamental and integrated systems research and testing will continue to generate improvements and

economic impacts felt by the general flying public as well as the aeronautics community.

The establishment last year of the Office of the Chief Technologist (OCT) enabled NASA to begin moving toward the technological breakthroughs needed to meet our nation's space exploration goals, while building our nation's global economic competitiveness through the creation of new products and services, new business and industries, and high-quality, sustainable jobs. By investing in high payoff, disruptive technology that industry cannot tackle today, NASA matures the technology required for our future missions in science and exploration while improving the capabilities and lowering the cost of other government agencies and commercial activities.

- In OCT's cross-cutting role, NASA recently developed draft space technology road maps, which define pathways to advance the nation's capabilities in space and establish a foundation for the agency's future investments in technology and innovation. NASA is working collaboratively with the National Research Council (NRC) to refine these road maps. The final product will establish a mechanism for prioritizing NASA's technology investments, and will support the initial Space Technology policy Congress requested in the NASA Authorization Act.
- As leader of the Space Technology program, OCT will sponsor a portfolio of both competitive and strategically guided technology investments, bringing the agency a wide range of mission-focused and transformative technologies that will enable revolutionary approaches to achieving NASA's current and future missions.
- In FY 2012, a significant portion of the Exploration Technology Development program is moved from

ESMD to Space Technology. These efforts focus on developing the long-range, exploration-specific technologies to enable NASA's deep space human exploration future. The integration of Exploration Technology activities with Space Technology creates one robust space technology budget line, and eliminates the potential for overlap had NASA's space technology investments been split among two accounts. ESMD will continue to set the prioritized requirements for these efforts and will serve as the primary customer of Space Technology's exploration-specific activities.

- OCT continues to manage SBIR [Small Business Innovation Research] and STTR [Small Business Technology Transfer], and integrates technology transfer efforts to ensure NASA technologies are infused into commercial applications, develops technology partnerships, and facilitates emerging commercial space activities

Education and Research

Recognizing that our work must continuously inspire not only the public at large but also students at all levels, NASA's education programs this year focus on widening the pipeline of students pursuing course work in science, technology, engineering and mathematics (STEM). As President Obama has said, "Our future depends on reaffirming America's role as the world's engine of scientific discovery and technological innovation. And that leadership tomorrow depends on how we educate our students today, especially in math, science, technology, and engineering."

- The FY 2012 request for NASA's Office of Education capitalizes on the excitement of NASA's mission through innovative approaches that inspire educator and student interest and proficiency in STEM disciplines. NASA's education program in FY 2012 and beyond will focus and strengthen the agency's tradition of investing in the nation's education programs and supporting the country's educators who play a key role in inspiring, encouraging, and nurturing the young minds of today, who will manage and lead the nation's laboratories and research centers of tomorrow.

- Among NASA's education activities will be a continued Summer of Innovation, building on the successful model piloted with four states this past year.

All of these activities place NASA in the forefront of a bright future for America, where we challenge ourselves and create a global space enterprise with positive ramifications across the world. The FY 2012 budget request provides the resources for NASA to innovate and make discoveries on many fronts, and we look forward to implementing it.

NASA's Future

As we enter the second half-century of human spaceflight, the nation can look back upon NASA's accomplishments with pride, but we can also look forward with anticipation to many more achievements to come. The NASA Authorization Act of 2010 (P.L. 111-267) has provided us with clear direction that enables the agency to conduct important research on the ISS, develop new launch vehicle and crew transportation capabilities to go beyond the bounds of LEO, utilize a dazzling array of spacecraft to study the depths of the cosmos while taking the measure of our home planet, improve aviation systems and safety, develop new technologies that will have applications to both space exploration and life on Earth, and inspire the teachers and students of our country. In developing and executing the challenging missions that only NASA can do, we contribute new knowledge and technologies that enhance the nation's ability to compete on the global stage and help to secure a more prosperous future.

These are tough fiscal times, calling for tough choices. The president's FY 2012 budget request makes those choices and helps NASA realize its potential and meet the challenges of the 21st century. We look forward to working with the committee on its implementation.

Viewpoint 5

> *"Five years ago the idea that the private sector might have been capable of transporting cargo and people reliably into low-Earth orbit was viewed as crazy."*

NASA Should Facilitate Further Privatization of the Space Program

Economist

The Economist *is a weekly newsmagazine. In the following viewpoint, the writer outlines the findings of the Augustine Committee, an independent review of NASA's space plans. The committee's final report recommends that NASA should outsource its transportation and cargo to private firms to save money for more ambitious goals. There are a number of private companies capable of taking over such responsibilities in the near future.*

As you read, consider the following questions:

1. What does the author say is the goal of SpaceX?
2. How much does it cost to launch a satellite costing only a few million dollars to build?

"Flying High," *Economist*, September 10, 2009.

3. According to the author, how much was SpaceX given to send cargo to the space station in 2008?

The past, despite the disclaimer often found on advertisements for financial products, often can be a guide to the future. In the early days of flight, the American government awarded a series of guaranteed contracts for carrying airmail. This stimulated the growth of air travel to the point where passengers could be transported affordably and reliably, and was the root of airlines such as United and American. Those who wish to travel into space argue that the government should now be doing a similar thing for spaceflight, with its aerospace agency, NASA, playing the role of the post office. This week [September 2009], there are signs that it might be about to.

The Augustine Report

At the behest of the president, NASA has been undergoing an independent review of its human spaceflight plans. On September 8th the review committee delivered a summary report. That the agency does not have enough money to return to the moon is no surprise. What is more surprising is that the Augustine report (named after the committee's chairman, Norman Augustine) argues that NASA should stop travelling to the International Space Station in particular and to "low-Earth orbit" in general. It should let the private sector do that instead, and focus its own efforts on more distant and difficult tasks.

Five years ago the idea that the private sector might have been capable of transporting cargo and people reliably into low-Earth orbit was viewed as crazy. Much has happened since, and two things in particular. One was that Virgin Galactic, an upstart British firm, said it would develop a space-tourism business based around a craft that had cost only $25m [million] to build. The other was that an equally upstart American entrepreneur called Elon Musk, flush from his sale of PayPal, created a company called SpaceX (whose Falcon rocket is pictured above, dropping its first stage on its way into orbit). He said he wanted to make it cheaper to launch people into space and wanted, ultimately, to send a mission to Mars—but that he would start by launching satellites.

We Have Liftoff

It would be an understatement to say that both ventures were treated with scepticism. But they have now come far enough to be able to thumb their noses at the cynics. On September 3rd SpaceX signed a contract worth $50m with ORBCOMM, a satellite-communications firm. The deal is to launch 18 satellites for ORBCOMM's network. Meanwhile, at the end of July, Aabar Investments, a sovereign-wealth fund based in Abu Dhabi, bought a 32% stake in Virgin Galactic for $280m. Aabar was not just interested in space tourism. It was also keen on a proposal to use Virgin's White Knight launch system to put satellites into low-Earth orbit. Will Whitehorn, Virgin Galactic's president, said that one of the things which attracted Aabar was the fact that White Knight (an aircraft which lifts to high altitude a rocket that can then take either passengers or satellites onwards into space) could be flown from Abu Dhabi.

Adam Baker of Surrey Satellite Technology, a British firm, knows a great deal about the economics of launching the kind of small satellites that Virgin's system might put into orbit. At the moment such satellites must either piggyback on the launch of a larger satellite or be launched rather expensively on their own rocket. A satellite costing only a few million dollars to build may thus cost $20m–30m to launch. Dr Baker says the challenge is to get the cost of a small-satellite launcher down to a few million, and he is so excited by the possibilities that he is leaving his employer to join Virgin Galactic.

The Role of Commercial Launch Vehicles

Commercial launch vehicles have for years carried all U.S. military and commercial—and most NASA—satellites to orbit. Now, as 50 years ago when we upgraded existing rockets for the Gemini program, NASA will set standards and processes to ensure that these commercially built and operated crew vehicles are safe. No one cares about safety more than I. I flew on the space shuttle four times. I lost friends in the two space shuttle tragedies. So I give you my word these vehicles will be safe. They will fulfill a critical NASA need, spur industrial innovation, and free up NASA to do the bold, forward-leaning work that we need to do to explore beyond Earth.

Charles Bolden,
Remarks at NASA Budget Press Conference,
NASA.gov, February 1, 2010.

Dr Baker reckons that costs can be cut if the launch rocket uses the satellite's guidance computer instead of having its own, and if the satellite's built-in rocket motor is bolstered to do the work now performed by a launch rocket's upper stage. That would mean satellite and launch rocket would have to be designed in tandem, so customers could not shop around for different launch vehicles. But Dr Baker is gambling that the system will be so cheap that this will not matter.

Using Private Firms

Over at SpaceX, developments have been just as interesting. Last year [2008] the company was given a $1.6 billion contract to send cargo to the space station. (Orbital Sciences, a firm that has been around since 1982, was awarded $1.9 billion to do the same.) This was the first time NASA had included private launch vehicles in its planning—the reality being that with the space shuttle about to retire the only other option was buying space on Russian rockets. The Augustine report now makes it more likely the government will dispense with NASA's services entirely in low-Earth orbit and ask private firms to deliver crew to the station, as well as cargo.

Implementing the Augustine Recommendations

Overall, the report is a healthy dose of reality for NASA. It warns that the agency's goals need to match its budget, and that it needs to internationalise its efforts, in order to make the most of its investments. For similar reasons the report tells NASA to extend the life of the space station. Abandoning the station in 2015, as is now the plan, would probably impair America's ability to lead international partnerships in the future. Spending a quarter of a century building something and then scuttling it looks bad, even if the useful science that has been done on board could be written up on the back of a postage stamp.

Finally, there is the moon. Should NASA go back? Mr Augustine's committee offers several possibilities. It does not rule out a return, but does describe something called a "Flexible Path" for exploration. This might involve sending people to the moon, but might also involve visiting asteroids and other places of interest. In other words, human exploration of the solar system does not have to be fixed doggedly on the moon first and Mars later.

Such flexibility sounds appealing. But in the case of NASA, which struggles to maintain funding for long-term projects because of short-term political juggling, it is a mixed blessing. If the committee's recommendations are implemented, the agency might still get much of what it wants, albeit more slowly than it would like. But there is a danger that without deadlines and an agreed budget, it will end up very rapidly going nowhere at all.

VIEWPOINT 6

> *"In fact, plans to privatize the U.S. space program are hardly unique to the Obama administration."*

It May Not Be Feasible to Privatize More of the Space Program

Carolyn Gramling

Carolyn Gramling is the web editor and a reporter for Earth Magazine. *In the following viewpoint, she suggests that current plans to utilize the commercial sector to do things like transport supplies, equipment, and people to the International Space Station or launch satellites have limits. Gramling quotes experts who believe that the space business will never be privatized—it will always be a partnership between NASA and the private sector. These experts argue that the private sector will always require government subsidies; that there are serious national security concerns; and that the lack of demand for such services will make NASA a major player in any business situation.*

Carolyn Gramling, "Bids in Space: When Should We Outsource Government Science?," *Earth Magazine*, June 30, 2010.

As you read, consider the following questions:

1. How many American firms got contracts in February 2010 to become part of a commercial space taxi industry, according to Gramling?
2. When does the author say that plans to create a commercial space market began to pick up steam?
3. What five countries does the author say received grants from NASA in 2010 to develop different aspects of the human spaceflight program?

Government research and development has its limits: Time, money and bureaucracy can all hamper the timely progress of research. As a result, many federal agencies are looking to private companies to help drive new innovation and keep costs down—but it's never that simple. Two current hot-button topics—returning humans to space and geoengineering—highlight a range of issues related to how private and public investment in science can coexist. This month [June 2010] we focus on NASA.

Paying for the Moon

When the U.S. budget briefings for fiscal year 2011 were held last February [2010], NASA's budget was one of the most eagerly anticipated. Rumors were flying that the agency might cancel the troubled Constellation program, an ambitious plan by the second [George W.] Bush administration to return humans to the moon by 2020. The still-under-construction Constellation program had fallen behind schedule and run over budget.

One basis for those rumors was an independent panel, commissioned by the [Barack] Obama administration in early 2009 to review the future of human spaceflight—and the fate of the Constellation program was one of the most urgent questions on the agenda. The fiscal year 2010 budget, announced in February 2009, had cut NASA's budget for human space exploration by $3.4 billion. Through 2020, Constellation would receive $80 billion, $28 billion less than NASA had expected when it devised the program.

After several months of review, the panel released its findings in September 2009: They found that the agency simply didn't have enough money to execute its existing human spaceflight plans. Given those limitations, the committee recommended using the commercial sector to defray its costs. It also recommended that NASA take a "flexible path" to develop new technologies that will ultimately take humans to Mars. Such a path would involve first exploring stepping-stone missions beyond low-Earth orbit, such as flybys of Venus and Mars and landing on an asteroid. But all of this will take money that NASA currently doesn't have.

In Search of Space Taxis

The fiscal year 2011 budget, announced by NASA administrator Charles Bolden earlier this year [2010], adopted many of the panel's recommendations and proposed to introduce major changes, not only to the agency's missions but also to its business model for developing new vehicles and other technologies. Under the new budget, the Constellation program would indeed be scrapped—and in addition, the three remaining, aging space shuttles would be retired in 2011.

Cutting those programs grabbed headlines. But it was the Obama administration's plan to outsource NASA's launch industry that really made news. As part of its proposed new direction, the agency announced it was seeking new private partners to develop spacecraft and technologies to take humans back into low-Earth orbit. In February, NASA awarded five American firms contracts totaling $50 million, in addition to two existing contracts totaling $3.5 billion through 2016—all to become part of a new, commercial "space taxi" industry.

These plans have met with vehement congressional and public opposition. In late February and again in March, Bolden defended NASA's budget proposal in hearings before the House committee on science and technology, whose members expressed fears that cutting the Constellation and space shuttle programs would result in job losses and over-reliance on the Russian Soyuz spacecraft to ferry astronauts to the International Space Station while the new launch vehicles were being designed. The committee also expressed deep reservations about the push for privatization of space technology: During the March hearing, Gabrielle Giffords, D-Ariz., noted that these changes "would make this country dependent on yet-to-be developed 'commercial crew' services of unknown cost and safety, with no government-backup system available." Regardless, the agency is moving ahead.

A History of Public-Private Partnerships

In fact, plans to privatize the U.S. space program are hardly unique to the Obama administration. NASA has been pondering how to create a commercial space market for decades, says Henry Hertzfeld, an expert in space policy at George Washington University in Washington, D.C. Those plans began to pick up steam after the loss of the space shuttle *Challenger* in 1986, which highlighted the need for additional types of spacecraft. Then, in the 1990s, NASA began to explore the feasibility of an alternate access program to supply the International Space Station. This led to the alternate access project, part of the Space Launch Initiative, a joint NASA-Department of Defense research and technology project to determine what new launch technologies would be necessary for the future of human spaceflight.

NASA commissioned a number of assessment reports on the topic by economists and private companies. In late 2005, then NASA administrator Michael Griffin made the case for privatization, stating that creating a competitive market would be more cost effective and, in fact, a financial necessity, if NASA were going to complete its mission to return humans to the moon by 2020. In 2006, NASA moved a little further forward with these outsourcing plans, creating the Commercial Orbital Transportation Services (COTS) program, which awards funds to private companies to develop vehicles that would deliver crews and cargo to the International Space Station. The next phase of this plan, called the Commercial Resupply Services program, awards contracts for the actual delivery of crews and cargo.

Two years later, in December 2008, NASA awarded COTS contracts totaling $3.5 billion to two companies—SpaceX (Space Exploration Technologies Corporation) and Orbital Sciences Corporation—to develop spacecraft that would supply cargo to the International Space Station. This funding marked the first time NASA had significantly outsourced a large chunk of a human spaceflight program to aerospace companies, rather than just using them as contractors. The five companies awarded grants earlier this year [2010]—Sierra Nevada Corporation, Boeing, United Launch Alliance (a joint venture between Boeing and Lockheed Martin), Blue Origin and Paragon Space Development Corporation—will be responsible for developing different aspects of the system that will launch crews into space, including upgrading rockets to make them safer, building a launch escape system and developing life support systems.

How Much More Can NASA Privatize?

All of this appears to create a trend of increasing privatization. But there is a limit to how much privatization can actually happen in this business, Hertzfeld says. He was one of the experts commissioned by NASA to write a 2005 economic analysis of the prospects for a commercial launch vehicle industry—and he did not take a rosy view of those prospects.

The Appeal of Commercial Spaceflight

"Our government space program has become overburdened with too many objectives, and not enough cash," says William Watson, executive director of the Space Frontier Foundation, a Houston-based group promoting commercial space activities. Watson said that allowing private companies to handle routine orbital duties could free up NASA to focus on returning to the moon and going to Mars.

Taylor Dinerman,
"NASA Approves Partial Privatization of the Space Program," FoxNews.com, May 11, 2009. www.foxnews.com.

"This [business] is not something that would ever become completely privatized," he says. "It will always be a partnership."

One reason, he says, is that the launch industry is a high-risk, high-capital business that needs heavy government subsidies to operate. Previous analyses of the commercial prospects for the use of space assumed that the cost of space travel would decrease over time—but historical trends don't bear that out; launching vehicles into space is as costly as it was in the 1960s.

But equally important, he adds, is the question of demand. Ultimately, the government is the top customer for these launch products, which means NASA controls the U.S. market. And NASA has specific requirements for safety and regulation that it must insist that its contractors adhere to. "For example," Hertzfeld says, "any time a vehicle gets close to the [International Space Station], NASA gets nervous, because it is a very expensive, delicate and important piece of equipment up there. . . . I don't think they're going to let the definition of what is safe lie totally in the commercial, private sector's hands. It is a question of who's taking the risk with the money to build [the vehicles]. And when push comes to shove, it's the government, because it's the government that needs the capability" to launch into space, he says.

When discussing the fiscal year 2011 budget, lawmakers have also expressed concerns that NASA's plan to further privatize might ultimately return the responsibility to NASA to complete a project, should a company building a vehicle fail mid-project for financial or other reasons, or fail to meet NASA's safety criteria. Administrator Bolden has responded to these concerns by stating that with more companies bidding to develop spacecraft, multiple companies might meet those safety criteria and provide necessary redundancy, so that at least one of them would succeed. But the question of whether NASA might be forced to step in to rescue a project—and pay the attendant cost—is still unclear.

All of these questions, Hertzfeld says, highlight why the launch industry isn't a business that can be fully privatized—because NASA can't afford to take the kinds of risks that come with a free market. "Price is not the allocator" for this business, he says, adding that aerospace companies have built plenty of launch vehicles—more than needed for current demands to launch payloads into space.

A Not-So-New Business Model?

During a speech at Cape Canaveral, Fla., on April 15, Obama noted that NASA has been relying on contractors for years, but now the agency is broadening the field "to make space more affordable." That affordability, he said, will be necessary if the U.S. is going to meet its lofty goals for human spaceflight—goals that the administration states include missions beyond the moon by 2025, first to an asteroid, and then to

Mars by the mid-2030s. To meet these goals, "we can't keep doing space exploration the way we've been doing it," he said in the speech.

But it is still unclear whether the Obama administration's plan will be economically feasible. And in fact, because NASA has always had partnerships with the private sector, which already builds the launch vehicles that NASA uses, the Obama administration's plans do not amount to a significant change in NASA's public-private partnership business model, Hertzfeld says. There are some differences: Historically, NASA has been very aggressive with setting the specifications and overseeing the production, and the new plan shifts—a little—"to letting the companies build and offer the services, for a price, to the government," Hertzfeld says. But it's not quite the same as a free market, he adds. Still, NASA administrator Bolden has echoed the Obama administration's sentiment that such changes are the best way forward in his own defenses of the administration's new plan. "We need a fundamental reinvigoration of the space effort," he said at the budget briefing in February. And NASA and the Obama administration are gambling that by drawing in private companies, that's what will happen.

Check back next month for another look at privatization: how private companies are investing in geoengineering research.

VIEWPOINT 7

> *"Teaching our students science, technology, engineering and math (STEM) has never been more important to innovating and competing in this global economy."*

NASA's Education Programs Should Be Better Funded

Jay Rockefeller

Jay Rockefeller is a US senator from West Virginia. In the following viewpoint, he opens a hearing on NASA's twenty-first-century challenges by discussing the impact that sporadic funding has on NASA's mission and priorities. Rockefeller criticizes the new budget for its severe cut to NASA's education programs, arguing that these programs help to inspire the next generation of American scientists and engineers.

As you read, consider the following questions:

1. What does Senator Rockefeller cite as some of the space shuttle's top achievements?
2. How many experiments have been conducted on the space station, according to Rockefeller?

Jay Rockefeller, Statement before the Senate Committee on Commerce, Science, and Transportation, March 15, 2011.

3. How much has been allocated for NASA education programs in 2012?

I would like to welcome all of our witnesses here this afternoon to discuss NASA's progress and challenges in implementing the NASA Authorization Act of 2010. No conversation on implementation, however, would be complete without also discussing the destructive impact that sporadic funding is having on NASA's mission and priorities.

NASA's Shifting Priorities

NASA continues to be an agency in transition. After 30 years and 135 flights, the space shuttle program is retiring. Just last week [March 7–13, 2011], we watched *Discovery*'s last mission. There is a great anticipation about what's next for NASA after the shuttle program comes to a close.

NASA's shuttle program has led to major scientific successes and discoveries. It's launched and repaired the Hubble Space Telescope, sent up the world's most powerful X-ray telescope, opening a window to the universe, and completed construction of the International Space Station. The space station is of particular interest to me—not necessarily because of what it teaches us about space—but because of the discoveries it's made that could improve the lives of every American. The shuttle also helped capture the imagination of a new generation of people too young to remember previous missions.

The space station itself recently passed a milestone of its own. Last November [2010] marked 10 years of a continuous human presence on the space station. Much of that time has been devoted to construction, but the astronauts on board still found time to conduct more than 1,200 experiments that supported the research of more than 1,600 scientists worldwide.

One very significant discovery is that some bacteria—such as *Salmonella* and methicillin-resistant *Staphylococcus aureus*

NASA's Education Programs

NASA's journeys into air and space have deepened humankind's understanding of the universe, advanced technology breakthroughs, enhanced air travel safety and security, and expanded the frontiers of scientific research. These accomplishments share a common genesis: education. As the United States begins the second century of flight, the nation must maintain its commitment to excellence in science, technology, engineering and mathematics education to ensure that the next generation of Americans can accept the full measure of their roles and responsibilities in shaping the future. NASA will continue the agency's tradition of investing in the nation's education programs and supporting the country's educators who play a key role in preparing, inspiring, exciting, encouraging, and nurturing the young minds of today who will be the workforce of tomorrow.

In 2006 and beyond, NASA will continue to pursue three major education goals:

- Strengthening NASA and the nation's future workforce,
- Attracting and retaining students in science, technology, engineering and mathematics, or STEM, disciplines, and
- Engaging Americans in NASA's mission.

"About NASA's Education Program," NASA.gov, 2011.

(MRSA)—become more aggressive in causing disease in the station's microgravity environment. I think everyone here is familiar with the enormous public health risk posed by antibiotic-resistant bacteria. Any progress we can make on this front will pay dividends for years to come. This discovery is helping scientists develop potential vaccines for both of these infections and, if successful, would save thousands of lives each year. For these reasons and for the scientific promise of future exploration, we need to get NASA's transition right.

Education Is Key to America's Future

Exploration, however, can take many forms and there is one area of the president's FY [fiscal year] 2012 budget request for NASA that particularly concerns me. That's the funding requested for NASA's education programs. The FY 2012 request is $138 million, which is nearly $42 million less than what was enacted for FY 2010. Teaching our students science, technology, engineering and math (STEM) has never been more important to innovating and competing in this global economy. In recent visits to schools in my own state of West Virginia, I have seen firsthand the success these programs have in inspiring our next generation of scientists and engineers. NASA's Space Grant [College and Fellowship] Program, for example, can be found in each and every state across the country. In my own state, the program funds fellowships and scholarships for students pursuing STEM careers at West Virginia University, Marshall University, and other colleges and universities around the state.

NASA's EPSCoR—or Experimental Program to Stimulate Competitive Research—is another education program working to improve STEM research and development in the aerospace field. In West Virginia alone over the past 5 years, this competitive program has supported hundreds of students and faculty in their research, resulted in millions of dollars in new funding, supported more than 100 scientific papers, and led to new patents. This type of program allows every state to fully participate in the research activities that lead to new discoveries, create new jobs and educate our workforce.

Periodical and Internet Sources Bibliography

The following articles have been selected to supplement the diverse views presented in this chapter.

Jessica Berman	"US Space Program Goes Commercial," *Voice of America*, April 27, 2011. www.voanews.com
Esther Dyson	"Enter the Dragon," *Slate*, January 20, 2011. www.slate.com.
Esther Dyson	"Liberating NASA," *Project Syndicate*, May 19, 2011. www.project-syndicate.org.
D.B. Grady	"One Giant Creep for Mankind," *Atlantic*, July 21, 2010.
William Harwood	"Obama Ends Moon Program, Endorses Private Spaceflight," CNET News, February 1, 2010. http://news.cnet.com.
Charles Krauthammer	"President Obama's NASA Budget Closes the New Frontier," *Seattle Times*, February 12, 2010.
Frank Mace	"In Defense of the Obama Space Exploration Plan," *Harvard Political Review*, April 7, 2011.
Katherine Mangu-Ward	"Space Cheese and Other Breakthroughs," *Reason*, December 17, 2010. http://reason.com.
Michael Palmer	"NASA Looks to Private Sector for Future of Space Program," NorthJersey.com, July 9, 2011. www.northjersey.com.
Rand Simberg	"Towards a Conservative Space Policy," *National Review*, February 1, 2010.
Debra Werner	"Garver: NASA Must Evolve the Way It Works with the Private Sector," *Space News*, July 29, 2011. www.spacenews.com.

OPPOSING VIEWPOINTS® SERIES

Chapter 4

What Role Should NASA Play in Diplomatic and Scientific Affairs?

Chapter Preface

Every day, tons of interplanetary material drifts down from outer space and lands on Earth's surface. Much of this debris is miniscule, like tiny dust particles released by comets far away from Earth or from asteroid collisions years ago. However, there are more substantial and dangerous objects that threaten to fall to Earth. The potential damage that a near-Earth object (NEO) can do is regarded by many scientists as a critical issue—one that requires concerted government action to protect life on our planet. NEOs are asteroids, comets, meteorites, and malfunctioning spacecraft that come into close proximity to Earth and its orbit. Obviously, a collision between Earth and even a relatively small NEO could have catastrophic consequences.

Of particular concern are near-Earth asteroids (NEAs), which NASA describes as "the bits and pieces left over from the initial agglomeration of the inner planets that include Mercury, Venus, Earth, and Mars." These large masses of rock and ice have been redirected by the gravitational attraction of other planets into the earth's proximity. Collisions not only have geologic consequences, but biologic ones. NASA assesses the danger from NEAs as a critical threat. "With an average interval of about 100 years, rocky or iron asteroids larger than about 50 meters would be expected to reach the earth's surface and cause local disasters or produce the tidal waves that can inundate low-lying coastal areas. On an average of every few hundred thousand years or so, asteroids larger than a kilometer could cause global disasters. In this case, the impact debris would spread throughout the earth's atmosphere so that plant life would suffer from acid rain, partial blocking of sunlight, and from the firestorms resulting from heated impact debris raining back down upon the earth's surface. Since their orbital paths often cross that of the earth, collisions with near-Earth objects have occurred in the past and we should remain alert to the possibility of future close-Earth approaches. It seems prudent to mount efforts to discover and study these objects, to characterize their sizes, compositions and structures and to keep an eye upon their future trajectories."

To evaluate NEAs and the threat they pose to human life on Earth, NASA has created the Near-Earth Object Program. NASA scientists identify, track, and characterize NEAs that might pose a threat years from now; since tracking began in 1995, the agency has discovered 8,033 objects of interest. NASA then determines the possibility of collision and figures out a way to deal with any problems years ahead of the estimated collision date. Such a plan would require international cooperation and participation. By 2020 the NEO program hopes to locate at least 90 percent of the asteroids and comets that approach the earth and are larger than one kilometer (about two-thirds of a mile) in diameter.

According to the NEO program, there are a couple of ways to deflect an NEA from a collision with Earth. One is a nuclear explosion set off near the asteroid to change the asteroid's velocity without fracturing it. Another option for intervention is placing large solar sails on an NEA so that sunlight could eventually redirect the object from its path.

Tracking and planning for NEAs and other threatening objects is just one of NASA's diplomatic and scientific projects examined in the following chapter. Other subjects include the controversy of NASA's diplomatic role, the future of the James Webb Space Telescope, and the launch of the Deep Space Climate Observatory.

Viewpoint 1

> *"In context, using NASA to reach out to the Muslim world doesn't sound all that crazy."*

NASA Should Recognize Its Diplomatic Role

Christopher Beam

Christopher Beam is a staff writer for Slate.com. In the following viewpoint, he highlights the truth in NASA chief Charles F. Bolden's recent statement that one of NASA's key goals is to reach out to the Muslim world and to celebrate its contributions to science, math, and engineering. Beam points out that diplomacy has always been essential to the NASA mission. Reaching out to Muslim countries represents an opportunity to foster greater collaboration, understanding, and cooperation.

As you read, consider the following questions:

1. When does the author state that NASA was created?
2. According to the author, the International Space Station was an opportunity for the United States to foster better relations with what countries?

Christopher Beam, "Earth to Conservatives," Slate.com, July 7, 2010. www.slate.com.

3. What does the author cite as NASA's annual budget compared to the Defense Department's budget?

Washington, we have a problem.

First, President Barack Obama whittled NASA down to a research center that oversees private spaceflight. Now he appears to have turned it into a subdivision of the State Department.

NASA and Muslim Outreach

On a visit to Cairo last week [June 2–July 3, 2010], NASA chief Charles Bolden gave an interview to Al Jazeera in which he said that Obama charged him with three missions: to "re-inspire children to want to get into science and math," to "expand our international relationships," and, "perhaps foremost, he wanted me to find a way to reach out to the Muslim world and engage much more with dominantly Muslim nations to help them feel good about their historic contribution to science, math, and engineering."

Conservatives were not over the moon. On Fox News, Charles Krauthammer called Bolden's comments "a new height of fatuousness. NASA was established to get America into space and to keep us there. This idea of 'to feel good about your past scientific achievements' is the worst kind of group therapy, psycho-babble, imperial condescension and adolescent diplomacy." At *National Review Online's The Corner*, Victor Davis Hanson questioned whether it's "really the business of a government scientific agency to produce historical and scientific narratives for political purposes." *Hot Air*'s Ed Morrissey argued that "Muslim nations should be insulted by the idea that the US pays NASA to provide them with paternalistic and patronizing validation and self-esteem boosts. And they probably will be."

Damage control ensued. A NASA spokesman told ABC that Bolden "understands that NASA's core mission is exploration." The White House threaded the two themes together, emphasizing that NASA should "engage with the world's best scientists and engineers as we work together to push the boundaries of exploration," including outreach to "many Muslim-majority countries."

Public Relations Is a Key Element of NASA

Bolden chose his words poorly when he said the goal was to make Muslim nations "feel good." But his statement revealed a truth about NASA that's rarely articulated by public officials: One of its main missions is now—and always has been—public relations. When NASA was first created in 1958, it served several purposes. The United States and the Soviet Union were engaged in a Cold War, so the space race was partly about defense—whoever controlled the skies controlled the world. But it was also symbolic: Landing on the moon before the Soviets represented the triumph of American technology and innovation. It was also an opportunity for the United States to win fans across the globe. There's a reason Neil Armstrong didn't call the moon landing one giant leap for the United States of America.

Ever since that first trip to the moon, though, NASA has struggled to justify its existence. There's still the defense justification: The only reason we're not speaking Russian now is that we didn't let the Soviets overtake us in space technology. But the real battleground has always been in the troposphere, not the thermosphere. There's the more benign scientific explanation: NASA pioneered breakthroughs in areas from experimental aircraft to satellite communications. Who knows what it may discover next? But it takes a lot of taxpayer money. There's also the romantic justification. In 2004, George W. Bush tried to recapture the glory of the 1960s by outlining a vision for astronauts to return to the moon by 2020. "Mankind is drawn to the heavens for the same reason we were once drawn into unknown lands and across the open sea," he

Why International Cooperation in Space Is Important

International cooperation in space exploration has the potential to provide significant benefits to all participants, particularly if managed well. Benefits in the form of monetary efficiency, programmatic and political sustainability, and workforce stability will accrue to those partners who choose to approach space exploration as a mutually beneficial endeavor. Furthermore, international cooperation must be explicitly incorporated as an aspect, and goal, of a modern space exploration program to enable coordination prior to the construction of new hardware. Such coordination can happen on both the government and industry levels and allows for advance planning and standardization that can enhance interoperability through the strategic use of redundancy. Finally, the promotion of a set of industrial standards for cooperation in space exploration will enable the exercise of leadership in future stages of the VSE [Vision for Space Exploration]. If the Vision for Space Exploration is to succeed, the United States, in particular, must engage its partners by reaffirming and strengthening its commitment to the International Space Station to maintain its diplomatic credibility for future exploration endeavors.

D.A. Broniatowski, G. Ryan Faith, and Vincent G. Sabathier, "The Case for Managed International Corporation in Space Exploration," Center for Strategic and International Studies, September 18, 2006.

said at the time. "We choose to explore space because doing so improves our lives and lifts the national spirit." Even Obama invoked President [John F.] Kennedy's moon shot during the

2008 campaign as an example of American industriousness. But again, $19 billion is a lot to spend on mechanical poetry.

Diplomacy in Space

That leaves the diplomacy justification. The Shuttle-*Mir* Program, a U.S.-Russia collaboration announced in 1993, fostered good relations between former rivals. The International Space Station was another opportunity for cooperation with Russia, Japan, and the European Space Agency. Obama puts even more emphasis on international relations. An administration report on national space policy released last week promises that exploration projects will help "all nations and peoples—space-faring and space-benefiting." It also assures allies that "there shall be no national claims of sovereignty over outer space or any celestial bodies." In more concrete terms, the administration's current plans for human space travel—a stop by an asteroid by 2025, followed by an eventual (and still very hypothetical) trip to Mars—would likely include other nations, and U.S. officials have reportedly reached out to China about joint space efforts.

In context, using NASA to reach out to the Muslim world doesn't sound all that crazy. Bolden may have put that goal in patronizing terms. But the core idea—that space efforts represent an opportunity for cooperation with countries in the Middle East—is a compelling one. Iran has a space program, as do Pakistan, Saudi Arabia, Turkey, and the United Arab Emirates. Inviting them to join the International Space Station or to collaborate on bilateral projects would be win-win.

That becomes difficult, of course, when administrations keep whittling away NASA's annual budget, which now stands at a measly $19 billion—a tiny slice of the Defense Department's $708 billion allotment. Perhaps the State Department can throw in a few extra billion.

VIEWPOINT 2

> *"Invoking the emotionally charged civil rights paradigm closes the door on nuance and context and encourages dogmatism."*

NASA Should Not Be Engaged in Muslim Outreach

Mona Charen

Mona Charen is an author and syndicated columnist. In the following viewpoint, she derides NASA chief Charles F. Bolden's announcement that one of NASA's main missions is to reach out to Muslims. Charen asserts that the goal of boosting Muslim self-esteem by celebrating Muslim scientific and technological advances is consistent with the Barack Obama administration's grandiose and unworkable ideas about the responsibility of government. She also finds NASA's outreach mission arrogant and "incredibly solipsistic."

As you read, consider the following questions:

1. Who is Muhammad ibn Musa al-Khwarizmi, as explained by the author?

2. What mental tic common to liberals does Charen believe that the Obama directive to NASA reveals?
3. According to Charen, does the Muslim world have low self-esteem that would benefit from NASA intervention?

It's not really surprising that President [Barack] Obama told NASA administrator Charles Bolden that his highest priority should be "to find a way to reach out to the Muslim world and engage much more with dominantly Muslim nations to help them feel good about their historic contribution to science . . . and math and engineering." It fits with so much that we already knew about the president.

It is consistent with his wildly exaggerated concept of governmental and presidential power and competence. Samuel Johnson wrote: "How small, of all that human hearts endure, that part which laws or kings can cause or cure." Obama believes the opposite—that his presidency can be a transformative moment not just for the nation, but for the world. He will halt global warming and stop the rise of the oceans, transition America to a green energy future, prevent the "cycle of boom and bust" in the economy, provide universal health care while spending less than before, cushion "underwater" mortgage holders without rewarding profligate borrowers, increase taxes on the "rich" without harming the middle class, solve the problem of excessive public debt by amassing more public debt and so on.

Boosting Muslim Self-Esteem

How in the world would NASA help Muslim nations to "feel good" about themselves? Would NASA hold science fairs in Tripoli or Tehran? Produce and circulate propaganda films about Great Muslim Men (careful, never women) of Science? Stress our global debt to Muhammad ibn Musa al-Khwarizmi, the father of algebra? (That's risky, since al-Khwarizmi reportedly learned his math from the Indians.) How would Obama's NASA chief undertake to alter the civilizational self-esteem of a billion people?

Of course, it's entirely possible (pace [author and critic] Bernard Lewis) that the Muslim world does not lack for self-esteem on the matter of science or anything else. Certainly, scientific know-how has not been lacking in nuclear-armed Pakistan or (would-be) nuclear Iran. Besides, hasn't Obama heard? The whole self-esteem myth has been exploded. Though millions of tax dollars and God only knows how many wasted instructional hours have gone toward making American kids think they are really, really special, it turns out that there is zero correlation between such drilled self-esteem and academic performance.

The Liberal Fallacy

The Obama directive to NASA also revealed a mental tic common to liberals—the tendency to universalize the African American experience. Just as African Americans were denied their rights and dignity, goes this reasoning, so today fill-in-the-blank are being persecuted or demeaned—women, gays, Muslims, the handicapped, illegal immigrants, Palestinians, "people of color."

But this line of reasoning impedes rather than advances understanding. The African American experience in America was actually very different from that of women, gays, the handicapped, illegal immigrants, or others *here*, to say nothing of the experience of Palestinians or "people of color" worldwide. Invoking the emotionally charged civil rights paradigm closes the door on nuance and context and encourages dogmatism.

To treat the Muslim world as a vast ocean of African Americans in need of respect and encouragement from us is both arrogant and incredibly solipsistic [extremely egocentric]. In fact, large swaths of the Muslim world feel inexpressibly superior to us—particularly morally and spiritually. Until cold terror forced them to accept American servicemen on their soil, the Saudis kept "infidel" pollution to the barest minimum in the home of the prophet. That wasn't an expression of inferiority. Osama bin Laden boasted in 2000 that he had defeated the Soviet Empire and that it would be a small matter to defeat the American one. Again, he may have been deluded, but he was not a candidate for assertiveness training. Nearly every Muslim child is instructed that his is the true faith, superior in every way to the errors that came before: Judaism and Christianity, and infinitely above paganism or atheism. Jihadis are taught that their shining pure religion requires no less than the mass murder of infidels and unbelievers.

It might just be that Muslim self-confidence is more dangerous to us than imagined Muslim feelings of inadequacy. But in any case, solicitude about the feelings of individuals cannot comprise a foreign policy. Muslim nations, like other nations, are motivated by advantage and influenced by perceptions of strength and weakness. The president has absolutely no control over the way Muslims feel about themselves—but he has every power over the way they perceive us.

Viewpoint 3

> *"NASA says [Administrator Charles F.] Bolden's comments are no big deal, and merely represent Bolden's attempt to reach out to his local audience."*

NASA Is Not Tasked with Muslim Outreach

Evan McMorris-Santoro

Evan McMorris-Santoro is a reporter and blogger for Talking Points Memo. *In the following viewpoint, he describes the controversy over NASA administrator Charles F. Bolden's comments that Muslim outreach is part of NASA's mission. McMorris-Santoro contends that an objective reading of Bolden's remarks shows that in no way does this mean that NASA is abandoning its key mission of space exploration and technological advancement, as some conservatives have charged. NASA officials argue that President Barack Obama believes that collaboration, cooperation, and outreach to the international community—not just the Muslim world—are essential aspects of the agency's mission.*

As you read, consider the following questions:

1. According to the author, what do right-wing commentators say Bolden's interview shows?

Evan McMorris-Santoro, "Right Wing: Oh Noes! NASA Doing Muslim Outreach," *Talking Points Memo*, July 6, 2010. www.talkingpointsmemo.com.

2. On what does Bolden say NASA's outreach mission is based?

3. What did NAA spokesperson Bob Jacobs say about Bolden's comments about Muslim outreach?

Have you heard? President [Barack] Obama has turned NASA into one big self-esteem booster for the Muslim world. At least that's what conservative commentators—who say they have proof Obama is ordering NASA to boldly go to the Middle East and make Muslims feel better about themselves—are saying today.

At issue is an interview NASA administrator Charles Bolden gave to Al Jazeera while on a trip to Qatar recently. The interview came as Bolden was in the Middle East to commemorate the one-year anniversary of Obama's Cairo speech, where he called for renewed ties between the U.S. and Muslim nations around the world. Bolden renewed the message of the speech, and said that NASA will be a part of forging the new path, thanks to a new focus on international engagement included in the Obama administration's space policy guidelines released last month.

The Controversy

NASA says Bolden's comments are no big deal, and merely represent Bolden's attempt to reach out to his local audience. But right-wing commentators say the interview is a sign that the only booster rockets NASA will be developing under Obama are the ones that lift Muslim spirits.

Bolden's comments show "Obama's lack of interest in American achievement or, indeed, American greatness," Paul Mirengoff at the *Power Line* blog wrote. They reflect "Obama foreign policy, which views American national greatness as an anachronism," wrote Elliott Abrams at the *National Review*. "Group and identity politics at its worst," Lou Dobbs said.

Examining Bolden's Comments

So, what did Bolden really say?

> "[In the 2009 speech, Obama] announced he really wanted this to be a new beginning of the relationship between the United States and the Muslim world," Bolden told an Al Jazeera English reporter when asked why he was in the Middle East giving speeches. "When I became NASA administrator . . . [Obama] charged me with three things: one was he wanted me to help re-inspire children to get into science and math, he wanted me to expand our international relationships, and third, and perhaps foremost, he wanted me to find a way to reach out to the Muslim world and engage much more with dominantly Muslim nations, to help them feel good about their historic contribution to science and engineering."

"It's not a diplomatic anything," Bolden added. "What it is is—it's trying to expand our outreach so that we get more people that can contribute to the things we do . . . there is much to be gained by drawing in the possibilities that are possible from Muslim nations."

Bolden suggested the idea was modeled on the existing International Space Station, which NASA constructed with modules built by countries like Russia and Japan.

Mischaracterizing Bolden's Comments

Over the weekend, right-wing blogs jumped on the interview.

"This is more evidence, if any were needed, of Obama's lack of interest in American achievement or, indeed, American greatness," Mirengoff wrote. "He seems to believe we've achieved enough (or perhaps too much) and that the trick now is to make nations that have achieved little for centuries feel like we couldn't have done it without them."

"Mr. Bolden should not be criticized for telling the truth about his job, for the problem is at the top, not at NASA,"

Abrams wrote at the *National Review*. "The space program is being transformed into a tool of Obama foreign policy, which views American national greatness as an anachronism."

By today, the story had become worthy of the full-on Fox News treatment. Lou Dobbs, who is a, you know, expert on both space and international relations, said the Al Jazeera interview means Bolden is "leading a sensitivity session as the administrator of NASA."

"This is group and identity politics at its worst," Dobbs said. "You don't have to be a space expert to know this is madness." . . .

Getting Caught Up in Political Rhetoric

The White House did not respond to my request for comment on the allegations that Obama's new plan for NASA put going into space behind making Muslims feel better. (Note: See Late Update below for the White House's take.) But NASA spokesperson Bob Jacobs told me that any suggestion that Bolden was describing a new mission for NASA in the interview was false. NASA will still spend its time exploring the cosmos and advancing aeronautics, he told me.

"I think unfortunately this has gotten caught up in some political rhetoric," Jacobs said.

Jacobs said he is "not aware" of any "specific efforts" to include Middle Eastern know-how in future space projects "at this point"—but said that since the Muslim world is "part of the international community," it made sense that Bolden would refer to the area when discussing the administration's plans to leverage international cooperation for the future of the space program.

"The interview took place in Qatar," Jacobs said. "I don't think it would be strange that he would make a specific reference to a local audience in his remarks."

Late Update

White House spokesperson Nick Shapiro writes in with this response to fear on the right that Obama's NASA is in charge of Muslim esteem rather than reaching for the stars. Shapiro said that Obama has "has always said that he wants NASA to engage with the world's best scientists and engineers as we work together to push the boundaries of exploration."

"Meeting that mandate requires NASA to partner with countries around the world like Russia and Japan, as well as collaboration with Israel and with many Muslim-majority countries," Shapiro said. "The space race began as a global competition, but, today, it is a global collaboration."

Viewpoint 4

"Out in deep space, [the Deep Space Climate Observatory] would do something that scientists are still unable to do today, directly and continuously monitor the earth's albedo, or the amount of solar energy that our planet reflects into space versus the amount it absorbs."

NASA Should Be Monitoring Global Climate Change with the Deep Space Climate Observatory

Bill Donahue

Bill Donahue is a writer and reporter. In the following viewpoint, he examines the controversy surrounding the Deep Space Climate Observatory (DSCOVR), an Earth-monitoring satellite that could have observed global warming in action. Instead, the project was shelved because of political opposition to the idea of climate change in 2001, under the administration of George W. Bush. It is commonly held that DSCOVR would provide the best scientific information on climate change, and its fate has been a loss for the scientific community. Donahue finds that there are efforts to bring it out of storage and finally get it launched in the near future.

As you read, consider the following questions:

1. When does the author say that the name of the satellite changed from Triana to the Deep Space Climate Observatory?
2. According to the author, what condition was DSCOVR in when a team of technicians and engineers examined it in 2009?
3. What country does the author say offered to send DSCOVR into space on a rocket?

It all began so hopefully. Al Gore proposed the satellite in 1998, at the National Innovation Summit at the Massachusetts Institute of Technology. Gazing skyward from the podium, the vice president described a spacecraft that would travel a full million miles from Earth to a gravity-neutral spot known as the L_1 Lagrangian point, where it would remain fixed in place, facing the sunlit half of our planet. It would stream back to NASA video of our spherical home, and the footage would be broadcast continuously over the web.

Not only would the satellite provide "a clearer view of our world," Gore promised, but it would also offer "tremendous scientific value" by carrying into space two instruments built to study climate change: EPIC, a polychromatic imaging camera made to measure cloud reflectivity and atmospheric levels of aerosols, ozone and water vapor; and NISTAR, a radiometer. NISTAR was especially important: Out in deep space, it would do something that scientists are still unable to do today, directly and continuously monitor the Earth's albedo, or the amount of solar energy that our planet reflects into space versus the amount it absorbs.

The Importance of Monitoring Albedo

We know some things about the earth's albedo. We know that solar radiation is both absorbed and reflected everywhere on Earth, by granite mountaintops in New Hampshire and desert dunes in Saudi Arabia. We know that cloud cover also reflects some of it. We also know that increased concentrations of carbon dioxide and other heat-trapping gases are currently causing the planet to retain more solar energy than it once did. But there is much we don't know, because we don't have a way to directly and constantly monitor albedo on a global scale—that is, to directly observe a key indicator of global warming.

To understand changes in the earth's climate, scientists rely on multiple and frequent readings of precipitation, temperature, aerosol and ozone levels, and a variety of other measurements, many of which are taken by Earth-monitoring satellites run by agencies such as NASA, the National Oceanic and Atmospheric Administration (NOAA) and the European Space Agency. But these spacecraft are all relatively close—at least 50 times as close as the L_1 point—so their utility is limited. No space agency has ever launched a satellite capable of seeing the whole Earth as a single, solar-energy-processing orb.

Triana

That's exactly what Gore's satellite was meant to do. He named it Triana, after Rodrigo de Triana, the sailor in Christopher Columbus's crew who first spied the New World. In 1998, NASA enlisted a 62-year-old physicist named Francisco Valero to lead in the design of Triana.

The agency expedited the program, with the goal of moving from conception to launch in three years, instead of the standard five or six. Giulio Rosanova, the mechanical-systems lead engineer for Triana, remembers bringing pepperoni rolls into work on Fridays, to cajole his crew of 15 into coming in on weekends. "We were excited," Rosanova says.

In those days, optimism abounded in NASA's earth sciences division. In a promotional video, the agency suggested that its planet-monitoring mission would extend beyond Triana—that a subsequent companion satellite would be dispatched to L_2, 930,000 miles away from Earth in the opposite direction, where it could constantly monitor the dark half of our planet. Together the two satellites would continuously watch the entire globe.

But in 2001, just a few months after the inauguration of George W. Bush, Triana's launch plan was quietly put on hold. "We were preparing to transport it to the launch site when we heard," Rosanova says. Instead, they wheeled the $100-million satellite into storage.

The Intrusion of Politics on Science

The mission entered a state of bureaucratic limbo. Around 2003, NASA renamed Triana the Deep Space Climate Observatory, or DSCOVR, but the satellite remained on the ground. During the Bush administration, it became politically vulnerable, largely because of its association with Gore. Dick Armey, then a Republican congressman from Texas, said of the satellite, "This idea supposedly came from a dream. Well, I once dreamed I caught a 10-foot bass. But I didn't call up the Fish and Wildlife Service and ask them to spend $30 million to make sure it happened." Despite the protests of independent scientists (including Paul Crutzen, an atmospheric chemist and Nobel laureate who wrote in a 2006 letter that "it would be a major waste of scientific effort and opportunity to discard such a meaningful mission"), NASA delayed the launch indefinitely.

Today, NASA officials aren't eager to talk about it. When I first wrote to the agency last summer [in 2010], I received a reply that made me feel like I'd asked about an unwanted pregnancy. "Currently DSCOVR is a mission without an agency," NASA publicist Sarah DeWitt wrote. "NASA still has no direction from anyone to fly the mission, so we don't really have anything definitive to say about its future as of right now." She suggested I contact NOAA, the other agency with a hand in the mission. When I did, the publicist there advised me to write to NASA.

So began my campaign. For the next eight weeks I would call, e-mail, and generally hassle various contacts at multiple agencies in a seemingly vain effort to see, with my own eyes, the only satellite that NASA has built but never launched.

The Need for DSCOVR

Since 1999, NASA and NOAA have been calling for an integrated Earth-observing system—a network of satellites that among other things, would consistently measure changes in the earth's climate. But that campaign is "languishing," said a 2010 Government Accountability Office report, and there are "significant gaps in future satellite coverage."

Meanwhile, Earth-observing satellites are subject to constant abuse. Cosmic rays grind on the delicate spectrometers that measure the planet's radiation. Over time, the satellites stray from their orbit and sink nearer to Earth. The data they collect becomes inconsistent. In short, they have limited life expectancies, and some of NASA's 14 Earth-observing satellites have already outlived theirs.

All of which makes DSCOVR's decade of dormancy more puzzling. In addition to the continuous macro-level monitoring of the earth's albedo that the satellite would perform, it could also be a crucial component of a larger satellite array. Because DSCOVR would be farther away from Earth than any other satellite, it would be able to see every other satellite in the sky. As a result, other satellites would be able to calibrate their location and sensors against DSCOVR. Moreover, because it would constantly face the moon, which has no atmosphere and thus a constant albedo, it would have a uniquely consistent baseline from which it could calibrate its instru-

> ### The Unique Capabilities of DSCOVR
>
> The instrument was to orbit the sun at the Lagrange point, where the combined—and oppositely directed—gravitational forces of the sun and the earth yield an orbital period the same as Earth's.
>
> This would allow the satellite to hold its position and provide the first direct, continuous measurements of solar radiation and absorption.
>
> *Molly Bentley,*
> *"NASA's Climate Science 'in Moth-Balls,'"*
> *BBC News, July 1, 2006.*

ments—and from which other satellites could calibrate as well. In this way DSCOVR could be the keystone on which present and future space-based Earth-monitoring systems could depend.

Such a network would fulfill the primary missions of both agencies. NOAA's mission is first and foremost to "understand and predict changes in the earth's environment." The National Aeronautics and Space Act of 1958, meanwhile, established NASA's first objective as the "expansion of human knowledge of the earth and of phenomena in the atmosphere and space." Yet for nearly a decade now, space exploration has been a higher priority for NASA than monitoring our own planet. Just this spring, it succeeded in pulling off a familiar-sounding mission: STEREO, in which a pair of satellites orbit the sun and beam back continuous footage of our resident star. But DSCOVR remained in storage.

Visiting DSCOVR

Last fall, my numerous entreaties to NASA were finally answered, and I was finally able to arrange a visit to Goddard

Space Flight Center [in Maryland] to see DSCOVR. Before I could get a glimpse, however, I was taken on a comprehensive tour that I couldn't help but suspect was designed to direct my attention toward a more positive narrative. First I met with Arthur Hou, the chief scientist for Global Precipitation Measurement (GPM), a multi-satellite mission that will start in 2013. Next my guide introduced me to the GPM's project managers. We all admired the shimmering metallic blankets that protect the spacecraft out in the cold, dark sky. Then the publicist gave me a GPM-branded coffee mug, souvenir ruler and license-plate frame. The detours continued. On the second morning of my two-day visit, I was guided into a theater and given special sunglasses, so I could behold Goddard's first-ever 3-D film. Eventually, though, I got my wish: a look at DSCOVR. Or rather, the box that contains DSCOVR.

Standing in a small, carpeted nook, I was able to look through a small observation window into a high-ceilinged, white-walled clean room where a white metal crate was shoved into a corner, beneath a stairwell. DSCOVR sat inside. A green tube supplied the box with a steady feed of nitrogen, to minimize contaminants. It looked to me like forgotten hardware—last year's cell phone gathering dust in a desk drawer.

Dick Cheney's Hand

It has never become entirely clear why the satellite had ended up here. In his 2009 book *Our Choice*, Gore wrote, "The Bush-Cheney administration canceled the launch within days of taking office on January 20, 2001, and forced NASA to put the satellite into storage." Warren Wiscombe, a senior physical scientist at NASA, blames a Bush-era "hostility" to earth science at NASA. "As to who ordered the axing of the mission," he says, "we'll never know, but the word we got was that Dick Cheney was behind it."

Mitchell Anderson, a Vancouver-based reporter who has obsessively covered the DSCOVR story, also suspects Cheney's hand, citing an unnamed NASA informant. Over the course of three years, Anderson filed five Freedom of Information Act requests for documents related to DSCOVR. After querying NASA in 2006, he waited 11 months to receive the documents. "They told me they were consulting with their lawyers," says Anderson, who was then writing for desmogblog .com. "When they finally e-mailed me the documents, they were scanned sideways. I couldn't read the top and bottom of the pages." The 70-page packet contained mostly letters that prominent scientists had written in defense of DSCOVR. All correspondence relating to the mission's mothballing was excluded.

In May 2007, six years after DSCOVR's original launch date was canceled, NASA convened 35 satellite specialists for a one-day workshop to decide to what extent DSCOVR would be able to replace the existing system of aging American satellites once they are decommissioned. The scientists agreed that the satellite has unique observational capabilities—the report the committee produced notes, "Sensors on the DSCOVR satellite have the potential to make important and innovative measurements from a novel perspective"—but they decided that it was not itself a suitable long-term replacement for an entire network.

Hal Maring, the atmospheric chemist who chaired the workshop, says that other satellite projects in the pipeline could do some of DSCOVR's work. NASA has a new low-Earth-orbiting mission, CLARREO, to be launched sometime in the next decade, and Maring says, "The [satellite] calibration capability offered by CLARREO will be much more useful than that possible with DSCOVR."

Wiscombe doesn't buy it. He says DSCOVR was stigmatized: "People called it GoreSAT, and NASA found people who would be the most hostile toward DSCOVR for the workshop. They handpicked the assassins."

The Rebirth of DSCVR?

Yet DSCOVR isn't dead. For all the talk of the satellite's cancellation, the 2009 federal omnibus budget bill, the first passed under the [Barack] Obama administration, contained $9 million specifically allocated "to refurbish and ensure flight and operational readiness of DSCOVR earth science instruments."

At Goddard, I met with Joe Burt, the lean and ebullient project leader for DSCOVR. Burt told me that in late 2009, a team of 15 technicians and engineers uncrated DSCOVR and found it in "outstanding" condition. "The propulsion tank hasn't lost a fraction of pressure after being put away for years," he says. "Everything mechanical on the satellite is working well. It's ready to go." He added that the two earth science instruments built for DSCOVR—EPIC and NISTAR—have recently undergone a $2-million refurbishment. "They're in fine shape," he says. "They're changing a couple of wavelengths on the filter. With different filters, you can see different things—different aerosols, different clouds. But it's not a big deal. Changing the filters is kind of like putting on a different pair of sunglasses." Burt says now that NASA has done the refurbishing, it could fly the satellite to L_1, as soon as 2014—if NOAA and the Air Force, which is interested in the effects of solar weather on its technology, provide the approximately $125 million to pay for the launch.

This all seemed like promising news until I visited NOAA, where I realized that interagency dysfunction still threatens DSCOVR's fate. At NOAA's headquarters in Silver Spring, Maryland, an assistant administrator named Mary Kicza told me that the climate instruments, EPIC and NISTAR, would be aboard the satellite when and if it launches. Then, speaking slowly, she said: "but earth science is not NOAA's purpose for the mission."

Instead, NOAA, like the Air Force, is interested in how the sun damages electronic equipment on Earth. It wants to equip DSCOVR with a coronagraph, an instrument that would monitor the plasma, particles and magnetic fields that stream out of the sun. Surges of plasma and magnetism can disrupt power supplies, short-circuit satellite electronics, and scuttle aircraft-navigation systems. "The goal," Kicza said, "is to send warnings back to Earth."

Politics Still Threaten DSCOVR?

What about EPIC and NISTAR? I asked. "Those instruments are part of NASA's program," Kicza said, "and you don't just flick them on. You need a ground system in place. You need algorithms developed." Are the algorithms developed? "For that," she said, "you'd really need to talk to NASA."

Sitting there, I feared that simple bureaucracy might yield a weird paradox—a Deep Space Climate Observatory mission that would do no climate observing.

The Story of Francisco Valero

Francisco Valero, the physicist who led DSCOVR's design team, is familiar with bureaucratic black holes. He is now 75 years old and retired, but he still actively tracks the fate of his creation. I figured that if anyone could accurately assess DSCOVR's chances of one day completing its mission, it would be him.

A few weeks after my visit to NASA and NOAA, I met Valero at his hilltop home in La Jolla, California. He has blood clots in his legs and related respiratory problems that sometimes leave him gasping for breath, but he was eager to talk. Sitting in his sparely appointed study, he explained how decades of research led him to imagine DSCOVR.

Valero fled his native Argentina in 1968 after a military coup. Amid widespread student protests, soldiers showed up at his university lab with machine guns to bar him from entry. He came to the U.S. so that he could do science at a remove from political uproar. Instead, he wound up in another kind of maelstrom. Since DSCOVR was shelved, Valero has persistently and publicly raised questions about the direction of NASA's earth science program, and he has questioned where funds earmarked for DSCOVR have gone. In 2004, when Ukraine offered to send DSCOVR to L_1 on a Ukrainian rocket—for free—Valero lobbied NASA to accept. "The satellite was built, the launch was free, and what did NASA say? The launch wouldn't be safe for the satellite." He shook his head in disdain. "I tell you, I lose sleep thinking about this stuff." Much of Valero's career focused on the effects that human activity can have on the earth's albedo, and when the opportunity to lead DSCOVR arose, he immediately recognized its potential. "With low-Earth-orbiting satellites, you can't get that," he said. "It's like you're reading a book with only one letter on each page. You can't get the whole story."

The Quest for Better Science

For Valero, DSCOVR isn't merely a satellite—it's part of the solution to one of the most pressing issues of our time. "We just need the truth," he said. "We need good science. If we get DSCOVR launched, we'll have that. And then the politicians will have something solid to base their arguments on."

Such persistent criticism, combined with long-festering resentments from scientists whose funding was redirected to pay for DSCOVR, has only earned Valero enemies at the agency. "He is hated at NASA headquarters," Wiscombe says. "His name is anathema there."

New Budget Priorities

But a week after my visit, it was widely reported that Obama's proposed 2011 budget would increase NASA's earth science budget by \$2.4 billion over the next five years. The funding would enable the agency to launch three Earth-observing satellites in 2011, including Glory, a delayed low-Earth-orbiting spacecraft that will monitor albedo, albeit not from the same privileged perch as DSCOVR would.

I called Valero to see what he thought of the news. He was guarded. "Is NASA's budget increase good news for DSCOVR?" he said. "I doubt it. Not in the present environment at NASA. They resist new approaches, and after spending decades and billions on traditional low-Earth-orbit satellites, they're too heavily invested to expand to new perspectives like L_1." He was silent a moment. Then his mood brightened.

"This satellite will fly someday," he said. "I have hope, for I think there's a beauty to science. It keeps asking questions. It demands answers, and it moves forward. DSCOVR represents the future. It has to launch, and it will."

Periodical and Internet Sources Bibliography

The following articles have been selected to supplement the diverse views presented in this chapter.

Dennis Bodzash	"White House: Improving Muslim Relations Not NASA's Job," *Cleveland Examiner*, July 14, 2010.
Ron Cowen	"Star Cents," *Science News*, April 9, 2011.
Jeff Crouere	"NASA: Muslim World, Here We Come!," *Slidell Sentry*, July 24, 2011.
John Getter	"Nothing New About NASA Outreach," *Houston Chronicle*, July 17, 2010. www.chron.com.
Jonah Goldberg	"One Giant Leap (Backward)," *National Review*, July 7, 2010.
Sarah Kendrew	"To Scrap the James Webb Space Telescope Would Be Short-Sighted," *Guardian*, July 11, 2011.
Ann McFeatters	"Is Selling State Services Responsible Policy?," *Naples News*, July 9, 2011.
Robin McKie	"NASA Fights to Save the James Webb Space Telescope from the Axe," *Guardian*, July 9, 2011.
Dennis Overbye	"Panel Proposes Killing Webb Space Telescope," *New York Times*, July 6, 2011.
Peter Pachal	"What We Could Lose if the James Webb Telescope Is Killed," *PC Magazine*, July 8, 2011.
Vin Suprynowicz	"Fallen Under the Rule of Lunatics," *Las Vegas Review-Journal*, July 11, 2010.
Byron York	"NASA's Muslim Outreach: Al Jazeera Told First," *Washington Examiner*, July 9, 2010.

For Further Discussion

Chapter 1

1. The first three viewpoints in the chapter explore the vision of the future for the US space program. After reading all three, do you feel the current direction of the US space program is the best one? What would you change and why?
2. In his viewpoint, Michael Lind asserts that human spaceflights should end. Russell Prechtl and George Whitesides argue that they should continue. Which viewpoint do you think makes the more persuasive case and why?
3. A number of scientists and space enthusiasts believe that a human landing on Mars should be a key priority of NASA. Read viewpoints by Loren Thompson and Iain Murray and Rand Simberg. Explain your position on the issue.

Chapter 2

1. In 2011, NASA's space shuttle program was officially grounded. Hanna Rosin reflects that the program has lost its magic. Pete Peterson points out that the shuttle program never performed to expectations. N.V. speculates that the private sector could take over the shuttle flights. Which viewpoint makes the strongest case? Why?
2. Where do you think the retired space shuttles should go? Ted Poe and Pete Olson contend that Houston should have gotten one, considering its importance as a hub of the aeronautics and space industries. Michael Grabois outlines the reasons why Houston did not get a retired space shuttle. Use information from the viewpoints to inform your argument.

Chapter 3

1. Newt Gingrich and Robert S. Walker assert that President Obama's NASA budget should be approved. George Landrith disagrees, contending that it should be rejected. After reading both viewpoints, what should Congress do about the NASA budget? Why?
2. The privatization of the space program is a hot topic in recent years. With the rise of space entrepreneurs and private sector involvement in space activity, many policy makers have debated the wisdom of letting for-profit companies take over vital missions and responsibilities. Read opposing viewpoints by the *Economist* and Carolyn Gramling. Is further privatization of the space program desirable? Explain your answer.

Chapter 4

1. Should NASA be involved in diplomatic outreach? Read viewpoints by Christopher Beam, Mona Charen, and Evan McMorris-Santoro. Explain your vision of NASA's diplomatic role using information from these viewpoints.
2. In his viewpoint, Bill Donahue reports that there is a movement to launch the Deep Space Climate Observatory after a number of years in storage. Why is the monitoring of climate change such a controversial activity?

Organizations to Contact

The editors have compiled the following list of organizations concerned with the issues debated in this book. The descriptions are derived from materials provided by the organizations. All have publications or information available for interested readers. The list was compiled on the date of publication of the present volume; the information provided here may change. Be aware that many organizations take several weeks or longer to respond to inquiries, so allow as much time as possible.

American Institute of Astronautics and Aeronautics (AIAA)
1801 Alexander Bell Drive, Suite 500, Reston, VA 20191-4344
(703) 264-7500 • fax: (703) 264-7551
e-mail: custserv@aiaa.org
website: www.aiaa.org

The American Institute of Astronautics and Aeronautics (AIAA) is the professional association of American aerospace engineers. The AIAA's mission is "to address the professional needs and interests of the past, current, and future aerospace workforce and to advance the state of aerospace science, engineering, technology, operations, and policy to benefit our global society." The AIAA created the AIAA Foundation to improve the education of aerospace professionals and has formed several technical committees for its members. The institute also publishes seven technical journals including the monthly *AIAA Journal*, which covers recent developments and initiatives in the field of aeronautics.

Christa McAuliffe Space Education Center
95 North 400 East, Pleasant Grove, UT 84062
(801) 785-8713
e-mail: director@spacecamputah.org
website: www.spacecamputah.org

Established in 1990, the Christa McAuliffe Space Education Center is a space education center that utilizes simulation to give students a realistic and exciting space experience. The simulators provide students insight into spaceflight, particularly the challenges of being an astronaut on the space shuttle. The center runs a highly regarded summer space camp for students all over the world and offers classes and field trips during the school year. The center's website features a blog that covers recent activities, programs, and breaking news. It also provides curriculum information for teachers who are interested in teaching students about space and space exploration.

Coalition for Space Exploration
website: http://spacecoalition.com

The Coalition for Space Exploration is a membership organization of aerospace companies that aims to "ensure the United States remains the leader in space, science and technology by reinforcing the value and benefits of space exploration with the public and the nation's leaders, and building lasting support for a long-term, sustainable, strategic direction for space exploration." The organization's website features the latest news, research, and commentary on NASA and space exploration; it also focuses on legislative efforts and initiatives, legislators' statements and testimonies, and policy briefs. The Coalition for Space Exploration provides resources for children and young people who are interested in science and space exploration, including contests for students K–12 and college.

European Space Agency (ESA)
8-10 rue Mario Nikis, 75738, Paris Cedex 15
France
+33 1 5369 7654 • fax: +33 1 5369 7560
website: www.esa.int

The European Space Agency (ESA) formulates space policy for the European Union. Its main mission is to enhance the European capability to explore space and add to human knowledge about our universe. The ESA also emphasizes the commercial possibilities in space; it works to promote technologies that benefit European industries and develop satellite technology that has commercial and security potential. Protecting the environment is also an aim of the agency, and the ESA works closely with NASA and other international space organizations to provide invaluable scientific information on Earth's environment. The ESA has a number of publications that are available on its website, including press releases, breaking news, training manuals, in-depth studies, and monographs. The *ESA Bulletin* is a quarterly publication that reports on recent projects and events.

Mars Society
11111 West Eighth Avenue, Unit A, Lakewood, CO 80215
(303) 980-0890
e-mail: info@marssociety.org
website: www.marssociety.org

The Mars Society is a nonprofit organization dedicated to the human exploration and settlement of Mars. The group fosters public outreach on the importance of human spaceflight to and settlement of Mars; lobbies for government-funded research on Mars; and facilitates private sector funding and involvement in Mars exploration. Another mission of the Mars Society is to develop the Mars Analog Research Station program, which was created to provide useful field research facilities for NASA and other space organizations interested in spaceflights to Mars. The organization's website has a video and image gallery as well as recent articles on Mars and the Mars Society.

National Aeronautics and Space Administration (NASA)
Public Communications Office, Suite 5K39
Washington, DC 20546-0001
(202) 358-0001 • fax: (202) 358-4338
website: www.nasa.gov

The National Aeronautics and Space Administration (NASA) was established in 1958 to develop America's space policy and oversee the country's exploration of the universe. NASA is a world leader in scientific research, which has enhanced the aeronautics industry and the private sector. The agency has been responsible for the Apollo program; the Hubble Space Telescope; the space shuttle program; and a number of other groundbreaking technologies and initiatives that have revolutionized our understanding of space and the origins of the universe. NASA publishes a quarterly newsletter, *News & Notes*, and numerous studies, in-depth reports, and news releases. NASA's website features a video and image gallery, congressional testimony and speeches, podcasts and vodcasts, blogs, and NASA TV, a TV station that plays NASA-related programs and video.

National Space Society (NSS)

1155 Fifteenth Street NW, Suite 500, Washington, DC 20005
(202) 429-1600 • fax: (202) 530-0659
e-mail: nsshq@nss.org
website: www.nss.org

The National Space Society (NSS) is an independent, nonprofit organization devoted to facilitating the human settlement of space and space exploration. The mission of the NSS is "to promote social, economic, technological, and political change in order to expand civilization beyond Earth, to settle space and to use the resulting resources to build a hopeful and prosperous future for humanity." To this end, the society lobbies Congress and raises funds to support its policies and advance legislation and policy pertaining to its goals. NSS publishes the *Ad Astra* magazine, a quarterly publication that covers subjects relevant to space exploration and settlement. The society's website also features position papers, congressional testimony, video and audio, press releases, book reviews, commentary, and general articles on space tourism, industry, settlement, and movement; Mars; and other topics.

The Planetary Society

85 South Grand, Pasadena, CA 91105
(626) 793-5100 • fax: (626) 793-5528

e-mail: tps@planetary.org
website: http://planetary.org

The Planetary Society is a membership organization made up of scientists, astronauts, entrepreneurs, educators, policy makers, students, business leaders, and space enthusiasts and is recognized as the largest public space exploration organization worldwide. The society funds projects like the solar sail, which is a spacecraft fueled by solar energy, and advocates for sound space policy and space exploration, including a mission to Mars. The Planetary Society also focuses on education about space exploration; students and space enthusiasts can read about a number of topics on the society's website. For children, the society provides a range of activities and educational materials, which are also available on its website.

Space Frontier Foundation (SFF)
16 First Avenue, Nyack, NY 10960
e-mail: info@spacefrontier.org
website: http://spacefrontier.org

Founded in 1988, the Space Frontier Foundation (SFF) is a volunteer advocacy organization dedicated to bringing about a permanent settlement in space. To accomplish this, the SFF recognizes the need for entrepreneurial spirit and action and the need for private-sector involvement in establishing space settlements. Therefore, SFF actively lobbies for the realization of "New Space," a term that refers to the merging of the free market and space policy and planning. SFF organizes conferences, seminars, contests, and awards to raise awareness of space policy and the commercial potential of space. The SFF website features a blog, a monthly newsletter, and access to breaking news, policy papers, and commentary.

Space Studies Institute (SSI)
1434 Flightline Street, Mojave, CA 93501
(661) 750-2774
e-mail: admin@ssi.org
website: http://ssi.org

Founded in 1977, the Space Studies Institute (SSI) is an organization that aims to "open the energy and material resources of space for human settlement within our lifetime. SSI's first commitment is to complete the missing technological links to make possible the productive use of the abundant resources in space." SSI has funded research on transport mechanisms, techniques to process lunar materials, retrieving and mining near-Earth asteroids (NEAs), and solar-powered satellites. It also organizes conferences and seminars and the publication of research papers on pertinent topics.

United Nations Committee on the Peaceful Uses of Outer Space (COPUOS)
Office for Outer Space Affairs
Vienna International Centre, Wagramerstrasse 5
Vienna A-1220
Austria
+43 1 260 60 4950 • fax: +43 1 260 60 5830
e-mail: oosa@unvienna.org
website: www.oosa.unvienna.org

The Committee on the Peaceful Uses of Outer Space (COPUOS) was set up by the United Nations in 1959 to review and foster international cooperation and collaboration in outer space exploration and settlement, to disseminate the exchange of ideas and information on outer space programs and initiatives, and to mediate conflicts between states that involve space issues. The COPUOS website provides updates on the committee's recent activities and concerns, a history of the committee, and an overview of the scope of its interests. It also features an archive of documents and reports and transcripts from past committee meetings.

Bibliography of Books

Robert S. Arrighi	*Revolutionary Atmosphere: The Story of the Altitude Wind Tunnel & Space Power Chambers*. Washington, DC: NASA History Division, 2009.
Joseph R. Chambers and Mark A. Chambers	*Radical Wings & Wind Tunnels: Advanced Concepts Tested at NASA Langley*. North Branch, MN: Specialty Press, 2008.
Eric M. Conway	*Atmospheric Science at NASA: A History*. Baltimore, MD: Johns Hopkins University Press, 2008.
Edgar M. Cortright, ed.	*Apollo Expeditions to the Moon: The NASA History*. Mineola, NY: Dover, 2009.
James Dean and Bertram Ulrich	*NASA/Art: 50 Years of Exploration*. New York: Abrams, 2008.
Paul Dickson	*A Dictionary of the Space Age*. Baltimore, MD: Johns Hopkins University Press, 2009.
Pat Duggins	*Final Countdown: NASA and the End of the Space Shuttle Program*. Gainesville: University Press of Florida, 2007.
Pat Duggins	*Trailblazing Mars: NASA's Next Giant Leap*. Gainesville: University Press of Florida, 2010.

Edward Clinton Ezell and Linda Neuman Ezell	*On Mars: Exploration of the Red Planet, 1958–1978: The NASA History*. Mineola, NY: Dover, 2009.
George R. Goethals and J. Thomas Wren, eds.	*Leadership and Discovery*. New York: Palgrave Macmillan, 2009.
R. Michael Gordon	*The Space Shuttle Program: How NASA Lost Its Way*. Jefferson, NC: McFarland & Co., 2008.
Brian Greene	*Icarus at the Edge of Time*. New York: Alfred A. Knopf, 2008.
Michael D. Griffin	*Leadership in Space: Selected Speeches of NASA Administrator Michael Griffin, September 2005–October 2008*. Washington, DC: NASA, 2008.
R. Cargill Hall	*Lunar Impact: The NASA History of Project Ranger*. Mineola, NY: Dover, 2010.
Roger D. Launius and Andrew K. Johnston	*Smithsonian Atlas of Space Exploration*. New York: HarperCollins, 2009.
Dillon S. Maguire, ed.	*Exploring the Final Frontier: Issues, Plans, and Funding for NASA*. New York: Nova Science Publishers, 2010.
Julianne G. Mahler	*Organizational Learning at NASA: The* Challenger *and* Columbia *Accidents*. Washington, DC: Georgetown University Press, 2009.

Harlen Makemson	*Media, NASA, and America's Quest for the Moon.* New York: Peter Lang, 2009.
Allan J. McDonald	*Truth, Lies and O-Rings: Inside the Space Shuttle* Challenger *Disaster.* Gainesville: University of Florida Press, 2009.
Michael Meltzer	*When Biospheres Collide: A History of NASA's Planetary Protection Programs.* Washington, DC: NASA, 2010.
Mike Mullane	*Riding Rockets: The Outrageous Tales of a Space Shuttle Astronaut.* New York: Scribner, 2006.
Martin Parker and David Bell, eds.	*Space Travel and Culture: From Apollo to Space Tourism.* Malden, MA: Wiley-Blackwell/Sociological Review, 2009.
Erik Seedhouse	*Martian Outpost: The Challenges of Establishing a Human Settlement on Mars.* Berlin: Praxis, 2009.
Erik Seedhouse	*The New Space Race: China vs. the United States.* Berlin: Praxis, 2010.
Tanya Lee Stone	*Almost Astronauts: 13 Women Who Dared to Dream.* Somerville, MA: Candlewick Press, 2009.

Index

C

D

E

F

G

H

I

J

T

U

V

W